MICHIGAN INTERNATIONAL BUSINESS STUDIES
NUMBER 15

RISK CONTROL
IN THE OVERSEAS OPERATION
OF AMERICAN CORPORATIONS

Donald L. MacDonald

Division of Research
Graduate School of Business Administration
The University of Michigan
Ann Arbor, Michigan

Library of Congress Cataloging in Publication Data

MacDonald, Donald L.
  Risk control in the overseas operation of American corporations.

  (Michigan international business studies; no. 15)
  Includes index.
  1. Insurance, Business.   2. Risk management.
3. Corporations, American—Management.   I. Title.
II. Series.
HG8059.B8M32   658.1′55   79-14011
ISBN 0-87712-193-1

*To the women in my later years—Millie, Marsha,
Marilyn, and Phyllis*

CONTENTS

PREFACE

Primarily, I intended that this book provide treasurers and vice presidents of finance with background regarding the difficulties encountered by employees who must cope with risks confronting their companies' foreign affiliates. Having acquired that information, presumably, officers will appreciate their risk controllers and will assist them effectively. I shall not, of course, seek court injunctions to bar others from reading the book.

In dealing with risk handling in operations abroad, I have not described the principles and basic practices of risk control. Other books, including one which I recommend heartily (out of self-interest), *Corporate Risk Control,* deal with such matters.

Although I would like to describe this book as an exhaustive study of conditions relating to risk control in all the countries in which corporations based in the United States have affiliates, I cannot do so. At my rates of speed in researching and writing, such comprehensiveness would have required twenty years of additional work. Therefore, I have described risk-related conditions in seventeen countries in which numerous American corporations operate large industrial plants or retail stores. Located in Europe, Latin America, and the Far East, the countries are reasonably representative of the areas of the world in which American corporations will be operating substantial units during the next two decades.

I did not include information relating to Canada, the country in which corporations based in the United States have established many more affiliates than in any other, for I feel that an entire book would be necessary to define the few major differences and the great many slight differences in risk-related matters in the two countries.

By including information pertaining to Mexico, I caused the title to be inaccurate; one need not cross oceans in traveling between the United States and Mexico. However, rather than discard a title I like, I included Mexico as one of the countries in the study and shall remind critics that overseas travel between the two countries is possible.

Throughout this book I have used the terms "risk control" and "director of risk control" in preference to "risk management" and "risk manager." A reason is my belief that man manages only man. His processes of direction of dogs, methods of marketing, portfolios of securities, and insurance programs, I feel, should be indicated by terms other than "managing." Another reason is my admiration for the hundreds of directors of risk control I have known over the past twenty-three years. The title "director of risk control" is more impressive than "risk manager" and is in keeping with the importance of the risk control function. However, I am not crusading, and if the benighted continue to use "risk management" and "risk manager," I shall not grieve.

The information and observations were provided by directors of risk control, brokers, agents, lawyers, managers and officers of industrial and mercantile companies, and employees of insurance companies. I am grateful indeed to the following people: Jonas Akerman, Richard Balotti, Theodore Bardage, Hein Barthold, Lloyd Benedict, L. Benich, D. M. Bettancourt, Fred Bielaski, H. Bolk, Thomas Brittan, Philip Brown, Jr., Harold Campbell, Don Carlson, Bjorn Christiansen, Harold Corbe, Michael Day, Russell Drake, Henry Devlin, Peter DuBorgh, Harry Fanjul, Peter Fornaca, Frederick Fort, Gregory Foster, Houghton Freeman, C. W. Gerheim, H. R. George, Alan Golightly, L. W. Goodwin, James Gormally, P. Gegnerault, Stephen Graves, J. S. Groene, C. E. Hadley, H. W. Heathfield, H. Gordon Heile, Horst Henrich, Arne Hilding, Ronald Hill, William Hollingsworth, George Holmberg, Bruce Howson, Richard S. Johnson, Jose M. Julian, Jerome Karter, Juan Katwiik, Martin Keller, Vitalano Kettlitz, Mateo Inurria, Everard H. Lee, James Leftwich, L. W. Lizzato, Kenneth Marlow, Terhune Marone, Hugo Marquard, Gareth Maufe, W. T. McEvan, Daniel Kervyn de Meerende, Rudolf Mees, C. H. Meyer, P. Moller, Kenneth Morgan, Christian Moulaert, Thomas Nygen, Leon Otte, D. H. Pantlin, Henry Parker, C. R. Patterson, Andre Pensis, Edwin Peters, Anthony Popple, Jose Camacho Prados, R. E. Pratt, Samuel Pray, Kenneth Price, Eldred Rausch, J. C. Regamey, Don Richards, L. Riggio, Juan Riveroll, A. E. Schwiezer, James Seatter, C. Shaw, Gunther Soppa, A. A. Smith, J. A. Smith, George Sterling, C. Stolk, Allen Stone, Harold Talbot, Richard Thompson, T. N. Trolle, C. Tryggve, Herbert Tugendhat, Walter Turner, A. M. Wikander, Luc deWilde, F. L. Wilkinson, L. V. Wilson, and L. Zetterman.

1

OUTLINES OF INTERNATIONAL
RISK CONTROL

Management cannot seek to profit by providing goods or services without facing the possibility that casualties will reduce earnings and deplete assets. Damage to property or theft may abruptly diminish flows of revenue and necessitate emergency expenditures. Liability to employees, customers, or others for damage to bodies, self-esteem, or property may drain off revenues and require changes which obstruct operations.

Profit lost through casualties or through uneconomic use of insurance reflects as unfavorably upon management as does the shrinkage in earnings from any other cause. Indeed, casualty-related reductions in profit reveal inadequacies in management more sharply than do losses caused by economic recessions. Therefore, management must work diligently and systematically to control the risk of loss of profits and/or assets through casualties. In particular, if a company operates foreign affiliates, management must shield it from casualties and the attendant high costs which reduce profitability.

Controlling risks of an overseas affiliate is more complicated than controlling risks in domestic operations. This chapter indicates the relationships which contribute to the complications and outlines organizational principles and practices conducive to coping with the problems generated by those relationships.

Throughout this study, a United States-based corporation which holds an ownership interest in a unit situated in another country is termed an "owner corporation," and the foreign unit, an "affiliate." The terms apply whether the ownership interest is whole or partial and whether the owner corporation exercises tight administrative control over the affiliate or virtually no control.

Purposes

Where risks of loss through casualties are controlled effectively, clearly defined purposes direct and prod those engaged in risk control. Ideally, top management recognizes the following purposes in both domestic and foreign operations:

1. Protection against significant reduction in profit margins
2. Increase in profit
3. Protection against loss of asset values so great as to cause severe dislocations

Management must emphasize the first two if risk control effort is to be directed toward the purpose for which the corporation employs capital and manpower, i.e., earning profit for distribution to its owners. Commonly it fails to do so, concentrating instead upon preventing reductions in assets. It thereby ignores the fact that use of assets is merely a means to the end of earning profit, and it exposes its company to possibility of faulty decisions. Having failed to view protecting profit as the foremost objective of risk control, it may, for example, decide to avoid the high cost of installing an automatic sprinkler system, relying instead upon insurance which would compensate fully for loss of asset values through fires. A disastrous consequence, if fire damage were to interrupt operations, however, might be a permanent loss of customers who, forced to buy from other suppliers during the interruption, would never return. In another situation, installing an automatic sprinkler system to prevent reductions in asset values might be financially dangerous; if the company's competitive position precludes the earning of substantial amounts for several years, amortization of the cost of installing sprinklers might remove any possibility of profit. More appropriate, probably, would be maintenance of insurance sufficient to replace or repair damaged facilities, to cover operating costs incurred during the restoration period, and to compensate for shrinkage in net earnings resulting from the interruption of operations.

Management does not have many opportunities to install risk control measures which contribute to increases in net earnings. Clearly, therefore, it must exploit every opportunity for increasing earnings as a top-level objective of risk control. It thereby requires those engaged in risk control to perform occasionally on the offensive team as well as to meet their usual defensive responsibilities. For example, when risk control personnel devise a system for minimizing pilferage of shipments en route from the company's plants in the United States to a proposed plant in another country and thereby clear the way for establishment of the foreign affiliate, risk control will have contributed to an increase in earnings for perhaps many years. Similarly, if accident prevention specialists introduce methods which permanently reduce the incidence of on-the-job accidents, the company's profits rise accordingly. And if management permanently reduces long-term costs of risk control by writing substantial deductibles into insurance policies, it contributes to increase in earnings.

While most persons in top management realize that to prevent reductions in assets brought about by casualties is a central objective of risk control, some are not discerning in their views of prevention. Any casualty-caused shrinkage in assets is undesirable, of course, but the shrinkages with which management should be most concerned are those so large that they cause dangerous economic stresses. A company in need of high-cost emergency loans to restore damaged facilities or to meet continuing expenses is in a position of stress, as is a company which has been denied such loans or one which has been unable to fill customers' orders because of the damage to its plant.

While consistency in the purposes and objectives in domestic and foreign operations ordinarily is desirable, differences in attitudes and history lead to differences in purposes of owner corporations and their foreign affiliates. Also, differences in the relationships between an owner corporation and such affiliates may preclude recognition of uniform purposes in all the foreign affiliates of an American owner corporation. Indicated below are mixtures of the three central purposes outlined above and others reflective of the varied conditions under which American corporations conduct operations abroad.

Purposes of Corporations Which Supervise Affiliates' Programs Closely

Some corporations shape and administer the risk control programs of their foreign affiliates. Many could do so but have decided against it. Many others are under agreements assigning responsibility for risk control to co-owners of the affiliates. The closeness with which a corporation is to supervise risk control in an affiliate affects its choice of purposes; if it is to exercise little or no control, it would accomplish nothing by establishing ambitious and detailed purposes.

A corporation is able to supervise risk control closely if it operates the foreign affiliate as a branch unit, if the affiliate is a domestic company and the corporation owns all or most of its stock, or if it is a minority shareholder but is under contract with the other owners to provide direction in risk control. In these three situations, use of the risk control purposes outlined above is practicable and productive.

A fourth major objective which may be useful is to build competence in risk control within the affiliate. When the owner corporation is constrained to exercise less control than its structural relationship with the affiliate would seem to permit, this tactic is essential. Illustrative of this situation is the position of a corporation which learned, shortly after buying control of a foreign company, that it could not retain the skills and experience of those who managed the company prior to the takeover unless it gave them almost as much authority in risk control and other areas as they had possessed formerly. Because management of the owner corporation had to give authority to the local managers even though it was aware that they had little knowledge of risk control, it adopted the fourth purpose.

Purposes of Corporations Which Supervise Affiliates' Risk Control Programs Minimally

Corporations barred from exercising managerial control over their foreign affiliates ordinarily do not formally define purposes in risk control. Relationships affording minimal degrees of control are these: joint ownership with a partner domiciled in the country of the affiliate which is responsible for overseeing risk control;[1] joint ownership with one or more companies of an affiliate which operates autonomously and is therefore answerable to its owners only in terms of net earnings; ownership of so small a fraction of a company's shares as to preclude participation in its management.

Even if a corporation cannot direct an affiliate's risk control programs, its duty to protect its stockholders requires effort to prevent decline in the value of its investment in the affiliate through ineffective risk control. Management acknowledges that duty in two ways: keeping informed on the quality of the affiliate's risk control system; moving subtly but persistently to induce the affiliate's risk controllers to adopt the basic three purposes indicated above.

Responsibilities in Risk Control Programs Closely Controlled by American Owner Corporations

Managerial failure to provide objectives for the guidance of those charged with control of risk in a foreign affiliate does not necessarily result in disaster; good luck may shield the affiliate from calamities. Chance also may permit it to survive another managerial oversight, i.e., failure to assign responsibilities in risk control. In the long run, however, the affiliate will incur needless casualties and spend excessively for insurance if the owner corporation's top management has not assigned responsibilities consistent with its purposes.

Risk control responsibilities, like purposes or objectives, differ according to the degree of authority possessed by the American owner corporations, by the other owners, if any, and by the affiliates. The sections below, therefore, examine separately the responsibilities delegated by top management of corporations that can closely supervise risk control operations in their foreign affiliates and the responsibilities delegated by managers lacking such authority.

Responsibilities of Top Management of Owner Corporations

If assignment of responsibilities in risk control is to be productive, top management must begin by recognizing its own responsibilities. While all in top management recognize the necessity of assigning responsibilities to subordinates, many do not set responsibilities for themselves. Specifically, they neglect to assume responsibilities in the three areas indicated below.

Self-education

The first responsibility of management is to learn enough about comprehensive and systematic risk control to appreciate its potentials, its costs and the barriers to its effectiveness. Management's take-off point in the acquiring of that knowledge is awareness that profit protection and increase in profit are the most important purposes of risk control. Managers who have become appreciative of those purposes are likely to seek information on the uses and limits of each of the basic devices of risk control, i.e., prevention of casualties, insuring and systematic loss absorption. Having gained such insights, they are equipped to make decisions relative to policy-making and operations in foreign affiliates. They can, with confidence, establish priorities, assign responsibilities, evaluate performance, and resolve disagreements between corporate directors of risk control and vice presidents, international.[2] Conceivably, they can contribute to the education in risk control of key employees of co-owners of affiliates.

Although the basics of comprehensive and systematic risk control are widely known, many in top management are unaware of them. Other executives—including some who supervise directors of risk control—know the basics are in print but are so lacking in interest that they do not seek them out. They fail to provide the highly visible support needed by their directors of risk control and make harmful risk control decisions. Under their supervision, risk controllers often are barred from making moves which would solve problems in their overseas affiliates.

Policy making

A responsibility of top management in the early planning of a new foreign affiliate is to require the planners to consider casualty prevention in the design of new facilities and in the hiring of its managers. In most corporations, unfortunately, top management does not recognize this responsibility. Consequently, the companies install preventive devices and layouts at high costs only after completion of construction of buildings. Typically, nationals hired to operate the new affiliate give no consideration whatever to casualty prevention in hiring production and maintenance personnel and in defining their jobs.

Incorporating fire controls into building plans is more efficient than installing such devices as automatic sprinkler systems, fire walls, heat vents, and access routes for fire control vehicles in buildings already in use. Consideration of employee safety when placing new machines is much less costly than relocating equipment after accidents, and hiring managers who know the potential for disaster through embezzlement is more economical than attempting to educate naive or indifferent managers on the job.

Another responsibility of top management in the process of establishing a new foreign affiliate is determining the amount of decision making to be given the affiliate. If management decides to grant full autonomy, it requires only that the affiliate report its major changes in risk control. If it chooses the other extreme, it places responsibility for planning and administration on the corporate director of risk control. If it divides authority, it permits the affiliate's management to handle matters such as selecting insurers and assigning duties in casualty prevention and makes the corporate director of risk control responsible for the rest.

Occasionally policy making in risk control is simple. If a prospective affiliate's management has little interest in the function and if the owner corporation employs effective risk controllers and needs to grant no special concessions to the affiliate, it assigns full responsibility to the corporate director of risk control. Conversely, it does not hesitate to grant complete control to an affiliate which employs competent practitioners in all areas of risk control.

Much more common, however, are complicated situations. An affiliate's management may be much less qualified to supervise risk control than the owner corporation but resents bitterly any restriction upon its authority; to sustain the managerial enthusiasm that has made the affiliate prosperous, the owner corporation grants autonomy in as many areas as is feasible. Risk control is one of the areas because uninformed managers assume that inferior performance therein cannot bring disaster. In another situation, top management acts on an assumption based solely on intuition. The vice president, international, insists that the affiliate's management remain in full charge of risk control because he feels that its knowledge of local conditions would be more useful than the broad experience of the corporate director of risk control.

Associated with assigning areas of responsibility is defining the relationships between the corporate director of risk control and the affiliate's management and its risk control personnel, if any. Ordinarily, top management states that the corporate director of risk control is a resource to be used by the foreign affiliate. It hopes that the affiliates' managers who are acquainted with the fundamentals of casualty prevention and insurance will expand their knowledge by studying the information he will provide. It hopes, too, that less knowledgeable managers will acknowledge their deficiencies and draw regularly upon his experience.

Ideally, in prescribing the relationship between the corporate director of risk control and an affiliate's risk controller, top management intends that the former will offer guidance in major matters and the latter will implement the recommendations or question them on the basis of his knowledge of local conditions. In defining the relationship between itself (the vice president, international, specifically) and the corporate director of risk control, management aims at assuring communication. It intends to ask for his advice and opinions and encourages him to initiate discussions.

In any area of international operations, corporate policy should include creating and maintaining a reputation for good citizenship in the affiliate's country. The implementation of this policy in risk control entails full compliance with laws requiring insuring in the domestic market. Although the owner corporation might be able to evade such requirements easily, a firm policy of honoring the law requires management to insure domestically despite such market inadequacies as undercapitalized insurers, low limits of protection, and outmoded policy forms.

No area of policy making relative to affiliates' programs of risk control requires more wisdom than indicating circumstances under which deviations from the corporation's risk control principles will be acceptable.[3] Management favors expediency in risk control no more than in any other function. Nevertheless, it recognizes that the corporation's interests sometimes are best served by deviating from principles. Thus, the vice president, international, insists on permitting an affiliate to insure through a broker who is the brother of its indispensible general manager, despite a corporate rule against buying services from relatives of executives. Another such deviation is the result of pressure on the owner corporation by local government to refrain from pressing charges locally against embezzlers.

Presumably, no company's management has written an employees' guide to expediency in decision making. Instead, management reveals its views through its actions. Thus, by castigating the corporate director of risk control for exempting an affiliate from bearing its share of the cost of a "world-wide" excess policy which the affiliate regarded as useless, corporate top management revealed its opinion of expediency under such circumstances. Clearly, management must react thoughtfully to such incidents, for its reactions will guide risk controllers in handling future problems.

Operations

A risk control responsibility of top management on the operations level is resolution of disagreements between persons involved in the control of affiliates' risks. However careful management may have been in describing employees' areas of authority, it may not have eliminated possibility of overlapping responsibilities which might generate disagreements. Ordinarily such disagreements in risk control need not cause top management much concern. Indeed, when the vice president, international, and the corporate director of risk control disagree, the other officers probably will never hear of it. Unless he is about to resign, the director of risk control does not contradict a vice president. When differences between the two do surface, either the vice president uses his authority to enforce his ideas or others in top management intercede. Because the vice president probably has deeper insights into the special problems of conducting operations in foreign countries, the authoritarian approach may well be the more suitable.

Settling important differences of opinion between the corporate director of risk control and the affiliate's management is a responsibility of the vice president, international, the member of top management to whom the director of risk control reports, or both.

If top management has ordered its director of risk control to supervise a foreign affiliate's risk control program, it should support him by requiring the affiliate's management to work with him. Ironically, the less interested the local managers, the more cooperative they are; having little enthusiasm for risk control, they do not resent his influence. However, resentful or not, they probably will give him minimum help unless corporate top management periodically makes clear its expectation of wholehearted collaboration in the cause of protecting profit margins.

If a manager had been the part-time risk controller long before the owner corporation's takeover, he may never be persuaded to give the corporate director of risk control much help. Even if he had devoted only a small portion of his time to buying insurance, he may so relish his reputation for shrewdness therein that he bitterly resents being assigned the role of in-house consultant. If, however, the corporate director of risk control must have local liaison, corporate management must either force the manager to help or assign the task to another employee of the affiliate.

Complementing top management's responsibility for backing the director of risk control by requiring affiliates to work with him is the necessity of providing financial support. Illustrative of supportive backing was the response of top management to a recommendation of the director of risk control that an affiliate buy its key supplier-company and make its buildings as fire and flood resistant as possible in order to raise the probability that the company will continue to provide essential components. The affiliate's management balked at making the expenditures, but corporate top management respected the opinion of the director of risk control that the supplier was exceptionally vulnerable to fire and flood and directed the affiliate to make the purchases. Top management of another corporation demonstrates its confidence in the director of risk control by funding his recommendation that the corporation's accident prevention engineers inspect the operations of each foreign affiliate annually.

Another important risk control responsibility of top management on the operations level is evaluation of performance. In both domestic and foreign operations, management encounters much difficulty in meeting this responsibility mainly because it lacks reliable indicators of success and failure. If it learns that man-hours lost due to job-connected accidents last year were approximately equal to the average for the preceding five years, it cannot assume that a new accident prevention program has accomplished nothing; installing new equipment and hiring 80 new employees who have difficulty understanding instructions probably offset the effects of the prevention program to some extent. Conversely, a reduction in insurance costs might not warrant commendation. Luck alone may have prevented the absorption of large amounts of loss under the deductibles which underlay the premium reductions and, in the coming year, absorbed losses may be many times greater than the reductions in premiums.

If top management can analyze and synthesize productively even when statistics are skimpy and if it has enough insights into the technicalities of risk control to estimate broadly the costs and benefits of risk control programs, it can draw realistic conclusions as to the effectiveness with which an affiliate's risks have been handled. At present, it cannot measure closely the values of efforts by the corporate director of risk control or by the employees of the affiliate.

Responsibilities of Owner Corporation's Director of Risk Control

If top management is free to supervise closely the risk control function in foreign affiliates, it usually assigns broad responsibilities to the corporate director of risk control. It does not, however, permit him to make the fundamental decision as to whether he should exercise full control. Neither does it permit him to make major changes in risk control programs on his own authority. Sensitive to the attitudes of affiliates' managers, it requires him to obtain approal for the proposed changes from them or from the vice president, international. Thus, he is primarily responsible for recommending changes and overseeing the administration of the affiliates' programs. Implicitly, he is also responsible for studying affiliates' insurance needs, the feasibility of their use of deductibles, and means of reducing the frequency and severity of casualties.

Obviously, if a director of risk control and his management do not recognize these responsibilities, he will contribute little to control of affiliates' risks. Less obvious is the fact that his contribution will fall short of potential if he does not assume other responsibilities. Outlined below are functions which management, because of its inadequate attention to risk control, commonly fails to regard as the responsibilities of the director of risk control. The highly effective risk controller compensates for this deficiency by assuming that they are his responsibilities.

Acquiring insights into attitudes affecting hazards

While top management expects its director of risk control to be well informed as to affiliates' hazards, it is not aware, ordinarily, of the amount of knowledge he needs of each affiliate's hazards. The superior director of risk control assumes responsibility for acquiring such insights. Consequently, he is engaged in an endless search for physical and mental conditions which can generate casualties. Occasionally, he detects attitudes capable of generating casualties. For example, he learns of judges who never find guilt in drivers who committed driving violations while driving their employers' vehicles. The judges' attitude negates the efforts of the affiliate to promote safe driving through education. In studying the operations of another affiliate the director of risk control learns that an accident prevention plan is ineffective because it is derided by the affiliate's foremen. Having gained such insights, directors of risk control can advise the affiliates to attack the damaging attitudes or to replace the plans.

Insights into attitudes lead also to effective insuring. If a corporate director of risk control were to accept the claim that "people are people" when it comes to thievery, he would urge all affiliates to insure against theft in the manner of the American corporation. However, study of attitudes may indicate that an affiliate's employees in one country regard stealing from their employer as a detestable crime, whereas they steal from other companies with great enthusiasm. Under the circumstances, the director would prescribe plans of insurance against embezzlement, robbery, burglary, and sneak thievery that would be quite different from those appropriate in the United States.

A major source of insights into attitudes affecting hazards are the flows of information maintained by insurance brokers. However, even the scattered offices of the major international brokerage firms differ widely in perception, knowledge, and breadth of foreign relationships. In seeking insights from brokers, therefore, directors of risk control must identify those best equipped to help them.

Education

Corporate directors of risk control have educational responsibilities beyond acquiring insights into hazards. They must add increasingly to their knowledge of problems and solutions in risk control, and they must educate others, some of whom have little desire to learn anything about the subjects. If they are to help managers plan and supervise risk control programs, they must search continually for information on such topics as behavior, law, fire prevention, engineering, and insurance markets. Only by educating managers of owner corporations and affiliates in the economics of risk control will they earn the all-important support of management.

Members of corporate top management who already know the elements of comprehensive and systematic risk control are informed by the director of risk control of new techniques in loss absorption, casualty prevention, and insuring. Managers who refuse to study risk control in other than its broadest aspects are likely to accept only data relative to proposals the risk controller is about to make.

If affiliates' managers are to work productively with corporate directors of risk control, they must regard risk control as a significant function of management, requiring skill and experience in research, analysis, invention, and administration. Moreover, they must be aware of savings possible through casualty prevention and systematic loss absorption. If their education has not included those subjects, they regard risk control as an assortment of processes worthy of only occasional moments of their attention.

Affiliates' employees who have been trained in risk control principles and techniques but lack knowledge of the owner corporations' attitudes toward casualty prevention and insurance usage and are unaware of the details of losses incurred by other affiliates are ill-prepared to operate risk control programs. Unless corporate directors of risk control educate them, they probably will never become effective risk controllers.

Building rapport

Another practice of risk controllers which contributes greatly to effectiveness in risk control is the creating and maintaining of rapport with key employees of owner corporations and their foreign affiliates. Clearly, a risk controller accomplishes more if he works with persons who are receptive to his ideas and want him to succeed than if he struggles with hostility, distrust, or lack of interest. While he can deliver information to persons antagonistic to him, he does not change attitudes and behavior unless he has established rapport with those he attempts to educate.

In addition to facilitating education, rapport enables the director of risk control to gain information and to implement his ideas. In particular, it helps him to obtain information on early planning which may affect affiliates' risks.[4] If his relationships with heads of departments such as marketing, legal, real estate, computer operations, finance, production, and transportation in the owner corporation produce a flow of news of plans which affect affiliates' risks, he can promptly raise questions and make suggestions. An episode illustrative of the benefits of such rapport began with a risk controller's early receipt of word of a plan to transfer to an affiliate's computer unit many functions previously handled by a time-sharing company. Believing that the new arrangement would invite embezzlement, he recommended that a set of procedures be introduced to discourage programmers, operators, and maintenance specialists from attempting to steal. Although the computer chief thought that such a precaution was unnecessary, his regard for the other's judgment caused him to endorse the proposal so strongly that top management put it into effect.

If rapport between the corporate director of risk control and the affiliate's management is lacking, the affiliate's risk control programs are much less effective than they might have been even though the risk controller's suggestions have been flawless and corporate top management has supported him strongly.

Assuming the initiative

Because changes in hazards, affiliates' capacities for absorbing losses, and conditions in insurance markets occur endlessly, risk control programs also must change. Corporate top management sometimes takes the initiative in making adjustments, but it does not spend enough time thinking about risk control to produce many of the ideas which lead to improvements. Moreover, it does not ordinarily include the making of proposals for modifying affiliates programs in the list of duties of the corporate director of risk control. Consequently, the risk controller must assume responsibility for undertaking the research which might point the way to improved programs.

In responding to that responsibility, he occasionally will discover that programs which he and top management had regarded as entirely satisfactory could be replaced with more effective arrangements. For example, he might come upon an indication that the most productive relationship between one of the affiliates and himself would be his serving it as a consultant on a fee basis.

Responsibilities of Affiliates' Managers

When the owner corporation is in close control of an affiliate's risk control function, the affiliate's management has few responsibilities in that area. However, its behavior in meeting those responsibilities largely determines the effectiveness of its risk control programs. One requires that it help the corporate director of risk control keep abreast of changes in hazards. This entails providing news of major organizational changes and requiring department heads to submit news of all risk-related developments in their units. To some extent, local management meets this responsibility by answering the questions of the corporate director of risk control, but its main duty is to volunteer news which it feels might be of interest to him.

It also is responsible for supporting casualty prevention programs conspicuously. Commonly, it bears this burden indifferently: while cost reduction is one of its major objectives, it cannot muster much interest in savings as difficult to document as casualties which have been prevented. By failing to convince rank-and-file employees that it believes that compliance with casualty prevention rules will result in significant savings, it dooms the programs to failure; unless such employees believe that the instructions are realistic, they will make only token efforts.

An undesignated responsibility of affiliates' managers is to oppose plans made by the owner corporations which they are certain would not be compatible with their companies' circumstances. Thus, a local management opposes a plan to secure all its insurance from American insurers because it knows that the move would so annoy its country's soundest bank—the owner of the affiliate's present insurer—that local financing thereafter would be more costly.

Responsibilities in Minimally Supervised Risk Control Programs

Responsibilities of Owner Corporation's Top Management

By choice or by the terms of the affiliation, a corporation may exercise little or no control over a foreign affiliate's risk control programs. Nevertheless, top management has responsibilities in such situations. The first, in point of time, is to keep informed as to the effectiveness of the programs. It does so by obtaining periodic reports from the corporate director of risk control. Another is its overriding responsibility for doing whatever is feasible to maximize earnings. Under this standard, therefore, it might decide to tolerate defects in an affiliate's risk control programs even though it knows that its corporate director of risk control could provide advice which would lead to major improvements. It would base its decision upon belief that resentment in the co-owner or the affiliate would exceed the risk control flaws in reducing profits. In another case of ineptitude of the co-owner or affiliate, management might decide that this most important of responsibilities—maximizing profits—would justify violating an understanding that it not interfere with risk control. Thus, it might withdraw control from the affiliate's management or demand the rewriting of a contractual clause specifying that the co-owner would have sole authority over risk control.

Responsibilities of Owner Corporation's Director of Risk Control

A corporate director of risk control has two responsibilities relating to an affiliate which operates autonomously or is under the supervision of another owner. If the affiliate or the co-owner requests advice, he must respond diligently. After ascertaining the nature of the problem, he provides advice in whatever detail is requested. The first of those two steps is likely to be the more difficult, for management of the co-owner or the affiliate may have so little knowledge of risk control that it cannot define the problem accurately.

The other responsibility is to monitor the affiliate for indications of the effectiveness of its programs. If top management does not instruct him to undertake such surveillance, he must propose to do so. In monitoring he refrains from offering gratuitous advice, but he presses firmly for issuance of periodic reports and accounts of changes. Occasionally, he obtains explanations and word of prospective changes in conversations with those in charge of risk control. Also, he questions outsiders, such as insurance brokers, whose ears are attuned to conditions within the affiliate.

Responsibilities of Affiliate's Management

An affiliate's only responsibility to its American owner corporation, if another owner is in charge of risk control, is the unvoiced obligation to know enough about the function to be able to contribute to the effectiveness of casualty prevention programs and to point out significant defects in its insurance policies.

Management of an affiliate which operates autonomously in risk control is, of course, responsible for equipping itself with knowledge of the elements of risk control. In addition, it has essentially the same responsibilities on the policy-making and operation levels as has the top management of an owner corporation which closely supervises risk control in its affiliates.

Installing and Modifying of Risk Control Programs

Top management makes its decisions relative to risk control in foreign affiliates under three kinds of circumstances: in the process of establishing new, single-owner units; while converting from partial to sole ownership; and under shared ownership. Described in the sections below are top management's principal areas of decision making under those circumstances. Indicated also are the chief roles of the owner corporation's director of risk control.

Under each of the three kinds of circumstances, the key factor in effective control of risk is a corporate director of risk control who is analytical, resourceful, experienced, and persuasive. Commonly, however, top management rejects the recommendations and proposals of risk controllers who are abundantly endowed with those qualities in favor of the ideas of managers of the affiliates who clearly are less qualified to prescribe risk control measures.[5] Usually, this action is provoked by a fear of the unpleasant consequences which may result from repudiating the ideas of the affiliates' managers. For example, top management has decided against implementing the recommendation of the corporate director of risk control that he closely supervise the programs of an affiliate even though the arrangement would be permissible and would result in reductions in insurance costs; behind the decision is the belief that the time is not ripe for top management to bruise the ego of the affiliate's managers by taking the risk control function from them.

Installing Risk Control Programs in Newly Formed, Single-Owner Affiliates

Ideally, top management makes two fundamental risk control moves early in the planning of a new foreign affiliate. The first, both in time and in importance, is to require the corporate director of risk control to recommend the casualty prevention features to be built into the new facilities. Mainly, he suggests measures for preventing long interruptions of operations by fires, explosions, employee injuries, or external happenings. Illustrative are the following suggestions made in the planning of a plant for making cement:

1. Change a plan to locate a hydrant a few feet from a bin in which clinker is to be cooled, lest accidental spraying of the clinker in attaching a hose while fighting fire cause an explosive creation of steam.
2. Design the kilns for quick conversion from the burning of coal to use of liquefied gas to avoid shutdowns in event of strikes by miners or railroad workers.
3. Build the plant eastward of the only nearby town, so that production will not be interrupted some day by court order following the filing of complaints of lung damage resulting from the fumes and particles carried from the smokestacks by the prevailing west wind.

Top management does not, of course, automatically include the risk controller's recommendations in the plans for a new affiliate. Its decision, however, may not be difficult; if the director of risk control has submitted adequate data, it can readily compare prospective costs and benefits. However, if he cannot predict with confidence the long-term value of losses to be avoided, management must base its decisions partly on speculation and partly on humanitarian considerations, i.e., the probability that adoption of the proposals would shield employees from burns, crushed limbs, poisoning, or other distressing on-the-job casualties.

Management's second move in the planning stage is to decide whether it will supervise risk control or grant autonomy to the affiliate. If it chooses the latter, it discards an opportunity for the corporate director of risk control to take charge with minimum damage to the egos of the local managers, inasmuch as they are likely to be too busy with other matters to resent the action. To withdraw control from the local management several years later would inevitably generate resentment.

About the only sound reason for placing responsibility for risk control wholly on an affiliate is that the affiliate has hired an experienced risk controller. Commonly, however, top management makes that choice for reasons that are less than sound.

Almost always, incorporating casualty prevention facilities into new buildings and assigning responsibility for establishing new risk control programs to corporate directors of risk control result from the initiative of risk controllers. With top management concentrating upon such topics in planning as construction costs, staffing, equipping, costs of production, and obstacles raised by government, it tends to overlook its responsibility for directing the risk controller to submit suggestions. The director of risk control, therefore, prods the appropriate member of management into recognizing the necessity of preventive planning and volunteers to establish the risk control programs.

Risk Control Moves in Purchasing an Established Company

Commonly, corporations based in the United States which share ownership of affiliates with companies domiciled in the affiliates' countries do not supervise the risk control programs, having agreed that either the domestic owners or the affiliates would be in charge of risk handling.

Upon converting from partial to full ownership or upon purchasing sole ownership of an established company, however, a corporation can do almost as it pleases with its affiliate's programs of risk control. If it chooses to transfer supervision to its director of risk control, significant improvement is likely. The affiliate's casualty prevention programs, if any, probably have been ineffectual, because of inexperience and inadequate funding. Its insurance policies may have been geared to the convenience of the insurance companies. A corporate director of risk control who is knowledgeable and skilled, works with specialists in the several areas of casualty prevention, and has the support of top management probably will improve the programs greatly.[6]

In exceptional situations, affiliates have operated comprehensive systems of risk control long before the American corporations attained complete ownership. Most of them have continued to handle their programs very effectively without help from their American owners. Their risk control personnel have deeper insights into local hazards than absentee risk controllers could have developed, and their knowledge of the views and attitudes of employees and customers likewise is superior. Consequently, they are well equipped to operate casualty prevention programs and to insure effectively.

Timing of transfer of control to owner corporation

If the director of risk control in a corporation which is to buy sole ownership of a company is much more skillful than the local management, logic decrees that risk handling should be transferred to him as soon as possible, i.e., when the company is purchased. Such timing, however, is unusual. Typically, following purchase of a company which had been independent in the past, the American purchaser's vice president, international, insists that the new affiliate retain full authority over risk control and various other functions in order to sustain local management's morale. Unwilling to argue with the vice president over a secondary matter during the busy period of tying the companies together, the other members of top management do not press for early transfer of responsibility for risk control. Even if they intend to centralize the function eventually, they may be so concerned with problems in other areas that they permit years to pass before they act. Nevertheless, a slow trend toward such centralization seemed to have developed by the mid-seventies.

Conditions underlying centralized risk control

Whatever the circumstances under which a corporation becomes sole owner of a foreign affiliate, top management tends to overlook the placing of responsibility for control of the affiliate's risks unless the corporate director of risk control prompts it to make the decision. Ordinarily, therefore, if top management has discouraged the offering of such reminders or if the corporate director of risk control believes that the affiliate is capable of coping with its risks, the affiliate controls by default.

The condition which is most likely to convince top management that its risk controller should assume control over risk handling in an affiliate is a high probability that centralization will increase the affiliate's earnings. The director of risk control may cause top management to anticipate such profits by pointing to other affiliates which have profited under his administration. His resourcefulness also may influence management: following the death of an affiliate's risk controller, he might point out the wastefulness of assigning risk control to an employee of the affiliate who is an experienced accountant, purchaser or other specialist. And following a competitor's ruinous fire, he indicates that an affiliate will remain exposed to a similar loss unless its fire prevention program is improved through centralization.

A plan for transfer of authority

During the early seventies, top management of a corporation which became the sole owner of numerous foreign companies during the fifties and sixties adopted a plan for placing the companies' risk control programs under close supervision of its director of risk control. In the first of the plan's four phases, he obtained permission from top management to arrange for a survey of an affiliate's insurance and casualty prevention programs by the corporation's international insurance broker or a correspondent broker in the affiliate's country. In the second phase, armed with the information provided by the brokers, he asked the vice president, international, to help by directing the affiliate's management to adopt risk control purposes which harmonized with those of the corporation, to obtain insurance policies which met those purposes, and to cover certain of its risks under the corporation's "world-wide" policies. In the third phase the risk controller visited the affiliates to discuss with their casualty prevention specialists the corporation's attitudes toward prevention and his recommended changes in the local programs. In reserve was the fourth phase: if the affiliate did not make the indicated changes in insurance and programs of prevention, the director of risk control revived the reform process by requesting permission to update his information by making another survey of the affiliate's risk control system. His hope for success in the second round rested upon obtaining findings so disturbing that the vice president, international, would place the affiliate's risk control programs firmly under the supervision of the corporate risk controller.

Influencing Risk Control in Affiliates Under Joint Ownership

As indicated above, most of the corporations based in the United States which own affiliates jointly with companies or individuals domiciled in the affiliates' countries do not attempt to supervise risk control, particularly if they hold minority interests and if the nationals own the insurers of the local companies. In such situations they confine themselves to attempting to influence decision making in selected issues.

Some corporations, however, do not thus defer to their co-owners. Their managers believe that they are obliged to maximize earnings from each investment, whatever the percentage of ownership; if they can increase the earnings of affiliates by supervising their risk control programs, they strive to win responsibility for the handling of risk even when they own only small portions of the companies' capital stock.

At least two methods have evolved which enable American corporations to exert influence in risk control in jointly owned affiliates abroad. One entails negotiating management contracts which hold the American owners fully responsible for risk control.[7] Ordinarily, the negotiating is a part of establishing the terms of joint ownership and reflects the bargaining advantage enjoyed by the buyer of the majority of the affiliates' shares. However, an American owner that holds a minority of a company's shares might serve under such a contract if the domestic owner's interest in risk control is not a product of a relationship with a domestic insurance company or if that owner appreciates the competence of the American director of risk control and the specialists who work with him.

Another means of providing inputs is a two-part process. The first step is a quiet comparison of losses through casualties incurred by the affiliate and similar companies in its country. Mainly, the director of risk control obtains the data from brokers. If the information indicates that those in charge of risk control need help, he obtains permission from his top management to present the data to the co-owner along with a statement to the effect that it is sufficiently disturbing to justify his employer's requesting that he be provided with periodic summaries of relevant developments and copies of the insurance policies.[8] Having gained at least grudging agreement from the co-owner or the affiliate, he moves in due course into the second stage. Its objective is to expand his beachhead of entitlement to information to a definite right to volunteer suggestions occasionally. Mainly, he argues that his having that right would not reduce the authority over risk control of the co-owner or affiliate (as the case might be), inasmuch as that company could reject any or all of his suggestions. His unvoiced expectation, however, would be that his suggestions would be implemented in approximate proportion to his company's share of ownership. If the corporation owned 50 percent of the affiliate's shares, that is, those in control would adopt about half of his suggestions.

NOTES

1. In many countries, the domestic owner corporations own insurance companies. Commonly, expediency leads the American companies to concede full control over affiliates' risk control programs to the co-owners.
2. Unfortunately, in making decisions in these several areas, management often must assign greater weights to irrelevancies than to its insights into risk control. It might, for example, have to discard a fire control proposal to isolate a heat-treating operation in an outbuilding because local management objects on aesthetic grounds. Similarly, it might refrain from urging use of large deductibles in an affiliate's insurance program because the co-owner also operates an insurance company which regards use of deductibles as a threat to the insurance industry.
3. Ordinarily, a corporation's principles of risk control are the product of experience and studies of the director of risk control and members of top management who have particular interest in the subject. Rarely, if ever, are they designated as principles. Instead, they appear in statements of objectives, in insurance manuals, in pronouncements in memos and letters as to acceptable costs-benefits ratios, and—above all—in management's acts and restraints.
4. This area of endeavor is a part of his responsibility (outlined in Chapter 2) to operate a news flow in order to obtain systematically the information needed to keep risk control programs attuned to changes in risks.
5. In most cases American career risk controllers are better equipped than employees of foreign affiliates to shape risk control programs. The level of appreciation in the United States of the value of in-house experts in casualty prevention and insuring is higher than in other countries. Consequently, talented persons have been encouraged to build careers in risk control.
6. Unless the affiliate's management knows that he is strongly backed by corporate top management, he may have only nominal control. The local managers may delay indefinitely in providing data he has requested and in making changes he has suggested. In the rueful words of a corporate director of risk control, "Without support, centralization simply won't work."
7. Sometimes such agreements are parts of packages of management contracts under which the American owners supervise such functions as research and development and employee benefits.
8. Ordinarily, in both stages, the director of risk control drafts the observations and proposals and the vice president, international, or another member of top management presents them. Otherwise, those in control would ignore them or put them aside for consideration in the distant future.

2

PROCESSES OF RISK CONTROL IN OVERSEAS OPERATIONS

In commercial and industrial operations in all countries, control of risk of loss through casualties begins with identifying the natural and man-made hazards which establish probabilities of loss.[1] Efforts of an American owner corporation to learn what hazards confront a foreign affiliate are complicated by differences between the two countries' attitudes, behavior, law, economic conditions, and natural environments. The first part of this chapter deals with means of fact finding.

Having recognized the hazards, management copes with them by developing and administering programs of casualty prevention, insurance, and systematic absorption of losses. The second section below outlines the conditions which prevail when risk control programs are highly effective and the conditions which preclude effectiveness.

The final section describes problems and methods of evaluating performance in risk control. A difficult enough function domestically, evaluation borders on the impossible in international operations.

Gathering Information on Affiliates' Hazards

In risk control, as in any corporate function, management cannot perform effectively if it lacks insights; it must know of each exposure to risk and each change in hazard. To acquire such knowledge, the director of risk control must monitor news of changes in the company's products, production methods, purchasing, marketing, transportation, buildings and equipment, and personnel. He must study preliminary plans for expansion or other major moves. He must search for early indicators of changes in legal climate, governmental restrictions and prescriptions, consumer attitudes, and economic conditions.

In operations within the United States, installing and administering systems for supplying directors of risk control with news are among the most difficult tasks in the area of communication. Plant managers, directors of marketing, directors of research and development, and other key persons are apt to be preoccupied with their main duties and to resent distraction; therefore they neglect to forward news items. Only if top management exercises all-important discipline does the director of risk control receive sufficient data to adjust controls to changes in risks.

But the special problems in obtaining news from foreign affiliates relate mainly to the degrees of control exercised by the owner corporations. Therefore, situations of close control and situations of little or no control are examined separately below.

In Closely Controlled Affiliates

Even though a corporation closely supervises the risk control operations of a foreign affiliate, it receives much less news of changes in hazards confronting the affiliate than of those confronting its domestic units. Almost no directors of risk control feel that they receive adequate flows of news of risk-related changes in domestic units. In comparison with the volumes of such news from foreign affiliates, however, domestic news arrives as an endless flood. Whereas twelve employees of a domestic affiliate might be dependable dispatchers of news, a part-time insurance administrator and a member of local management might be the only reporters in a foreign affiliate. Moreover, its employees may be unable to make their reports in English. The corporate director of risk control must then depend upon translators, who may provide distorted versions of developments unless they have considerable knowledge of the hazards.

Even if a corporate director of risk control routinely receives news from foreign affiliates, he may be handicapped by major omissions. Dispatches of an overseas administrator may be edited by superiors determined to prevent the owner corporation from learning of events suggestive of managerial shortcomings. Moreover, external developments—such as the courts' new leniency toward thievery and their awarding of large damages at the expense of manufactures—may not be recognized as hazards by either the administrator or the management. Quite possibly, such environmental changes will pose more difficult risk control problems than changes within the affiliates.

A corporate director of risk control in regular correspondence with an able local counterpart who has broad access to risk-related news and is not censored by an apprehensive management probably receives an adequate flow of internal news. He is particularly well supplied if the local director of risk control works with a risk analyst who gathers and interprets news from all divisions of the company. He may not, however, receive sufficient news of external developments to be held fully accountable for the effectiveness of the risk control function.

To compensate for that deficiency, he can draw upon the knowledge of insurance brokers and companies. Typically, he hires the services of an American brokerage firm which maintains an office in the affiliate's area or of a domestic broker who is associated with a respected American broker.[2] Specialists in such firms are aware of the broad social, economic, and legal changes which bear upon hazards. Some are skilled in ferreting out news regarding companies' employees. American insurance companies and associations of insurers maintaining offices abroad are less willing than brokers to study the hazards of companies which they are not insuring. However, they inform their policyholders of hazardous developments.

In Affiliates Minimally Controlled

Under contracts with their affiliates or with the co-owners thereof, many corporations based in the United States have little or no authority over the foreign risk control programs. The management of such corporations usually does not attempt to keep closely informed of changes affecting the affiliates' hazards. Some managers, however, believe that their duty to protect stockholders' investments requires alertness to such changes even if co-owners oversee the risk control programs.

A corporation which has no voice in an affiliate's risk control operations cannot monitor changes in hazards by directing the affiliate to inform it of significant developments, nor can it expect the co-owner or the affiliate's management to provide monthly compilations of such news. It can, however, request periodic summaries of changes in the risk control programs and the reasons therefor without being charged with interference. Also, it probably would not violate the hands-off agreement if its director of risk control were to obtain information on changes in hazards through periodic discussions with lawyers and bankers in the affiliate's country and by purchasing brokers' investigative services.

The latter two means of gathering information are quite costly. Unless management knows how wasteful inept handling of risk is and realizes the impossibility of detecting ineptitude without examining risk control measures in the light of the hazards to which they relate, it does not authorize buying such services. As a consequence, the corporation is among the many who make no effective effort to keep abreast of changes in affiliates' risks.

In addition to using the above methods, some owner corporations try to improve the fact-finding techniques of the co-owners or the affiliates. Ordinarily, room for much improvement exists; systematic intracompany transmittal of risk-related news is a rare practice. If improvement is to occur, the corporation's director of risk control must educate in two stages. In the first stage, he must awaken the controlling management to the fact that systematic gathering of information is the foundation of risk control. The task is difficult because the managers probably have little interest in any aspect of risk control and because he has no authority over the affiliate's risk control function. Since he cannot bombard the managers with instructional material, he must educate them subtly, creating opportunities to describe the spectacular improvements in risk control achieved by companies by establishing effective news flows. Thus, he tells the owner corporation's vice president, international, of a company which had profited substantially by basing its risk control operations upon systematic fact-finding; and thus the vice president recalls the illustration during a meeting with managers of the co-owner or affiliate, impressing them with the possibility that the affiliate could benefit similarly.

In the second stage of his educational effort the corporate director of risk control provides guidance in building the affiliate's information system. Again, because the relationship between the companies precludes his volunteering such help, he must employ indirection. Ideally, he will induce the affiliate's management or that of the co-owner to request assistance in organizing a news flow. Again, he depends upon members of corporate top management to tell the affiliate's managers of his skill in developing such systems.

Casualty Prevention

Understandably, but ironically, management of a company which has survived a costly casualty commends itself for its foresight in having insured adequately or prepared for absorption of the blow. A much higher level of achievement would have been to prevent the casualty, for loss is waste however complete the insurance cover or however appropriate the plan of systematic loss absorption. Management can condone such waste only if the costs of prevention exceed the value of casualties avoided.

Many in management regard casualty prevention as an incidental part of risk control; because this view is much more pronounced abroad, any American corporation must assume that the nationals who manage its foreign affiliates have no interest in prevention. Most of them would ridicule suggestions that they spend more on casualty prevention than on insurance. They ignore recommendations to expand preventive activity from conducting rudimentary programs of fire prevention to use of systems of engineering for controlling fire, explosion, power failure, collapse of structures, rupture of fuel or water lines, injurious accidents, theft, damage to goods in transit, or loss of valuable employees. Few consider preparing plans for coping with such casualties as destruction of plants or interrupted flows of parts from suppliers crippled by damage or strikes.

Behind the lack of interest in casualty prevention overseas is belief that managers waste their talents if they turn their attention from sales or production to secondary (or tertiary) matters. Moreover, several areas of risk are not at all menacing in most countries.[3] In many countries, for example, so few product liability suits are filed and such small amounts of damages are awarded that expenditure by manufacturers of large sums for the prevention of injuries to users of their products is not warranted. Another factor has been the insignificant reductions in premium rates which insurance companies have awarded for installation of automatic sprinkler systems and other devices for control of fire. If amortization of the cost of installing an automatic sprinkler system via fire insurance savings requires twenty-five years, the ratio of cost to benefits is acceptable only to those few managers whose view of risk control includes the values of losses prevented.[4]

Conditions Conducive to Prevention of Casualties

Given the general undervaluing of casualty prevention abroad, widespread ineffectiveness is inevitable. The condition, however, is not universal, for some affiliates operate programs superior to those of their American owners. Indicated below are circumstances underlying particularly effective systems of prevention, classed according to the relationships between the American owner corporations and their affiliates.

In affiliates wholly owned by American corporations

Essential to prevention in a wholly owned affiliate is authority held by the corporate director of risk control to communicate directly with the affiliate's management relative to each area of prevention. While he cannot demand undue amounts of management's time, he must be free to make significant recommendations and evaluations directly. If his messages must move through intermediaries, questioning and explaining which would have contributed to the managers' understanding of preventive programs will not occur. Moreover, indirect communication delays adjustment to changes in hazards.

Another element of effective systems is the belief of the vice president, international, that casualty prevention is productive; and in addition to knowing that prevention reduces insurance costs and shields employees and others from painful injuries, he recognizes that it can produce valuable secondary benefits. For example, a method for reducing pilferage by employees could add enough to net earnings to reduce employer's rate of interest for bank loans. Likewise, a dramatic reduction in the injuries in a foundry which has long deserved its reputation for maiming employees might attract more productive workers than those who had tolerated the more dangerous conditions.

Ideally the affiliate's chief executive would regard casualty prevention as an essential function of management. He would be aware that substantial savings can be accomplished through prevention. He would weigh costs against prospective savings in the distant future as well as in the next year or two. He would support prevention programs so conspicuously that some of his zeal would be implanted in employees on all levels.

Finally, and all important, is effective communication between the owner corporation's specialists in prevention and those who administer the affiliate's programs. The base of such communication is periodic face-to-face discussion. Thus, the corporation's accident prevention engineer spends a month or more in first-hand study of the affiliate's problems. He learns of strengths and weaknesses, particularly in attitudes of employees who have prevention responsibilities. The employees draw upon his knowledge and, above all, learn that his judgment is sound. This two-way learning is augmented by communication via telephone and mail.

The most important product of a communicative relationship is encouragement of the affiliate's management to seek help routinely from the owner corporation's specialists. However intuitive the specialists and however informative their occasional visits, they cannot anticipate all problems. Consequently, local managers must ask early for assistance in coping with particularly difficult problems.

In large jointly owned companies

A few of the American corporations which share ownership of large foreign affiliates with other corporations direct casualty prevention operations under contracts with the co-owners. Ideal conditions in such situations are essentially those described in the preceding section. In many more cases, contracts between the American corporate owners and the co-owners place full responsibility for risk control on the affiliates. In such situations of autonomy, the ideal circumstances are those indicated below.

Most important is an affiliate's management which believes that prevention is the main element of risk control. Such managers know that almost all forms of insurance are designed to apply to direct losses only and that policyholders therefore must absorb secondary losses, such as slovenly workmanship by employees who become contemptuous of their employer as they watch fellow employees embezzle with impunity. These informed managers spend for prevention even when earnings are low. They also spend sometimes for purposes regarded as frivolous by the unenlightened. As an example, a company might hire a psychologist to construct personality profiles of employees before assigning them to jobs which might be dangerous for persons subject to extreme absent-mindedness or irritability.

Another desirable condition in the affiliate is employment of a full-time director of risk control who shares the same comprehensive view as his counterpart in the American owner corporation. He is familiar with the problems and the basic techniques of each area of prevention and is his company's expert in at least one of them. Mainly, however, he observes and evaluates the work of specialists and seeks funds for improving programs. He regards the American owner corporation's director of risk control as the proprietor of a clearing house of information from which he occasionally can obtain ideas. Accountable only to management of his company, he can reject suggestions offered by the owner corporations without fear of losing his job or becoming a pawn in struggles between the owners for control of casualty prevention. Each owner honors the affiliate's autonomy, requiring only that it receive periodic reports.

Contributing greatly to the effectiveness of the casualty prevention program controlled by an affiliate are administrators in prevention who have supervisory responsibilities in related fields. Thus, the superintendent of plant maintenance is in charge of fire and explosion prevention, an in-house auditor oversees the program of embezzlement deterrence, and an engineer who works mainly in quality control also administers the programs under which products which might harm users are withheld from the market.

Working with such supervisors are prevention specialists. Ideally, each is as knowledgeable as the person doing the same work in the

American owner corporation. The specialist in fire prevention continually studies the chemistry and physics of fire and searches for insights into hazards peculiar to his country and his company. Like the local director of risk control, he is accountable only to his company's management and knows that his experience and ability are appreciated. Because he is not supervised by foreign management, he does not hesitate to propose changes in the program of prevention.

In small jointly owned companies

Almost none of the small companies which are owned jointly by American and domestic corporations employs either a full-time director of risk control or specialists in casualty prevention. The American co-owner of such a company best compensates for this lack of local expertise by directing preventive operations under an agreement with the co-owner. Its casualty prevention specialists design the programs and work with local management in administering them. Local management forwards news of important changes affecting prevention. Also, it oversees the performance of employees who have responsibilities in the programs: for example, it prevents shipment of fragile products in cracked styrofoam containers for shipment, for however shock absorbent the containers are when intact, they will not prevent damage if they have been cracked.

Ideally, the small affiliate's management participates in casualty prevention because it believes that systematic prevention is profitable. In reality, however, it may be only going through the motions of participating, having inherited the assumption that expenditure of time or money on casualty prevention is wasteful.

To supplement the news relating to prevention which is provided only spasmodically by local management, the American owner corporation obtains information from brokers or insurance companies. Mainly, it draws upon them for information on environmental conditions of which local management is unaware and for comparisons of its affiliate's performance in prevention with that of other domestic companies. Ordinarily, it pays for the information by buying insurance through the brokers and from the insurance companies which provide the information. Therefore, it must choose the brokers and insurers which are to provide the affiliate's insurance.

Conditions Unfavorable to Casualty Prevention

The ideal conditions outlined above for operation of casualty prevention programs in foreign affiliates occur rarely. More typical are obstructions frustrating to corporate directors of risk control. In many cases, American risk controllers are able to exercise so little influence that programs succeed or fail by chance. Indicated below are some of the techniques used with occasional success to surmount the obstructions.

The most common obstruction is the barring of the American corporation's specialists in prevention from volunteering advice to the affiliate or requesting detailed data as to effectiveness of programs. Ordinarily, the vice president, international, imposes the prohibition, believing that the intrusion would not be worth the annoyance it might generate in the affiliate or in the other owner. He informs the affiliate's management that the corporate director of risk control will provide preventive services upon request, but management usually ignores the invitation. Only if the vice president has learned that the prevention specialists can enable the affiliate to save enough money to warrant incurring some resentment in local management is he likely to lift the restriction. Armed with that belief, he may be able to smooth ruffled feathers by reminding management and, if necessary, a co-owner that casualties prevented must be equated with profits.

Some American owner corporations are prevented by contract from interfering with affiliates' prevention efforts, with control assigned to either the domestic owners or the affiliates.[5] Even under such restriction, however, the American director of risk control can at least obtain information on changes in the affiliate's hazards and on its preventive measures. He can interpret such data and, if permitted the expenditure, can study some of the programs in person and buy studies of others. Also, he may be able to obtain information from employees who have visited the affiliate for purposes unrelated to risk control: in talking with a chemical engineer who has helped the affiliate install a new production process, he learns of a need to protect employees against skin and eye damage; similarly, in conversation with an employee who has worked with the affiliate in planning construction of a new building, he learns that the public water supply is inadequate to prevent a calamitous fire. Through these means of obtaining information, the corporate director of risk control can detect deficiencies in programs and devise remedies. While the affiliate's management may shrug off most of his suggestions, self-interest will force it to implement some.

Whether or not an American company shares ownership of its foreign affiliate, lack of experience on the part of the affiliate will impair the effectiveness of prevention operations. If not forced to hire specialists, the affiliate assigns prevention to employees whose other tasks allow time for it. Ordinarily, in such a situation, the owner corporation must rely on the affiliate's consulting prevention engineers provided by American brokers or insurers. Unfortunately, while the brokers and insurers make their fire control technicians available in many countries, they send very few engineers abroad to assist manufacturers in preventing distribution of defective products which might injure customers.

An outsider specializing in fire prevention cannot, of course, issue directions to the affiliate, but he may be able to offer suggestions without affronting management. In talking with the superintendent of warehousing who is responsible, more or less, for fire prevention in storage buildings, a fire control engineer points out the logic behind his suggestion that a no smoking rule be strictly enforced. Had the discussion not occurred, the superintendent would have continued to ignore the rule, partly because of reluctance to deprive laborers of a source of comfort and partly because no fires had occurred in the warehouses during their decades of existence. The engineer may not have created a commitment to prevention, but his accounts of cigarette-caused fires which destroyed warehouses, of loss of jobs following fires, and of the explosiveness with which the contents of the buildings would burn will result at least in closer enforcement of the smoking ban.

Limitations in Exportability of Casualty Prevention Techniques

Owner corporations have wasted money in attempts to use prevention methods abroad which were designed to meet conditions in the United States. Having employed a domestic program successfully, management naturally hopes to maximize benefits by using it abroad. However, installing such a plan in another country in disregard of environmental differences is a mistake, for it can prove useless. Illustrative is exporting a program for control of employee pilferage that trains supervisors to detect tension in their subordinates which might indicate intent to steal. The program has enabled management to detect numerous thefts by neophyte embezzlers in the United States, but it would be worthless in a country in which the only nervous pilferers are youths in their first few weeks of employment.

Possibly, too, a foreign affiliate would not need a program which has been successful in the United States. In the United States, for example, a corporation might estimate that it has saved approximately $90,000 annually under a plan for preventing damage to its autos by careless employee drivers. The plan requires a checklist examination of each vehicle upon its return to the motor pool. In a country where employees regard driving as a skilled trade and greatly admire expensive motor vehicles, however, driver carelessness is not a problem.

To avoid wasteful exportation of techniques, therefore, the owner corporation's director of risk control must ascertain whether or not the conditions accounting for the effectiveness of plans in the United States are closely matched in the affiliate's country.

Insurance Usage

Owner corporations do not have to convince the affiliates' managers of the need of insurance. To most managers abroad, insurance usage and risk control are synonymous. However, awareness of the value of insurance does not necessarily produce insurance programs satisfactory to American directors of risk control. With affiliates or their domestic co-owners in control of insuring, the programs commonly reflect views very different from those held by the corporate directors of risk control. (Indeed, even some programs controlled solely by the American corporations represent managerial attitudes differing from those of the risk controllers.) Out of the various patterns of control emerge insurance programs which, from the standpoints of American management, range from inferior to superior. The first section below describes conditions producing inferior programs. The second outlines conditions within each of the patterns of control which produce superior programs.

Conditions Underlying Inferior Programs

The inferior programs of many companies owned jointly by domestic and American corporations can be blamed upon the American companies' yielding control over insurance when they purchased their interests. Granting such control is appropriate when a domestic owner is at least as well qualified as its American partner to oversee the affiliate's use of insurance. If, however, the domestic owner lacks insurance expertise, the move may result in inadequate protection and excessive premiums.

Some of the domestic corporations which control the insuring of jointly owned affiliates have obtained their concessions in order to profit through conflicts of interest. They own insurance companies or owe money to banks which own insurance companies and are at least as interested in maximizing the revenues of the insurers as in minimizing the costs of the affiliates' insurance. Therefore, they require the affiliates to insure with their companies or with those of their banks whether the premium rates and the protection are advantageous or not.

A form of counterproductive behavior stemming from nationalism causes domestic owners to refuse to permit affiliates to draw upon the experience of the American owners. Even if an affiliate does not have an insurance administrator and the American corporation employs specialists who have solved the insurance problems of affiliates in a dozen countries, the domestic owner may demand that the specialists play no part in planning or administering the affiliate's insurance program. Consequently, the program may have defects which should have been prevented. For example, it may include no supplementary policies, even though the American owner can document survivals of huge losses due to excess policies. Typically, the domestic owner justifies such obstruction by claiming that he (or the management of the affiliate) perceives changes in hazards promptly and is in close association with brokers and insurers in the domestic market.

However, whether ownership of companies rests entirely with corporations based in the United States or is shared with domestic companies, governmental attitudes are the principal causes of defects in many insurance programs. Governmental interference in use of insurance is the subject of Chapter 7; this section notes only that nationalistic intent to protect domestic insurance industries and urgent need of premium tax revenue are formidable obstacles to effective insuring. These conditions spawn restrictions such as forbidding insurers in the domestic market to offer policy forms which would appeal only to affiliates of American corporations. Government thereby eliminates any possibility that such forms would provide American interests with insurance superior to that used by domestically owned companies. Also illustrative is a requirement that the insurers in the domestic market secure their reinsurance from domestic reinsurance companies or governmental facilities. With those reinsurers able to provide only low limits of protection, the insurers are unable to provide the amounts of insurance American owners might want to apply to their affiliates. Under such regulation, highly effective insuring may be impossible.

An error commonly made by American companies in controlling the insurance programs of their wholly owned affiliates is the pressing of overseas insurers to insure for much larger amounts than they can provide without strain. Instead of buying the amounts used by domestic companies (augmenting them, if necessary, with excess covers), such owners insist upon policy limits higher than the levels acceptable to the insurers. They thereby antagonize the insurers and sometimes force them into reinsurance contracts with alien insurers which are both expensive and hazardous.

A similar mistake is demanding that an overseas insurer use the policy forms applicable to the owner's American operations. Desire for protection under familiar forms and phrases is universal, but winning assent to use them does not guarantee security. Overseas insurers and courts have interpreted phrases and clauses developed in the United States quite differently than American owners, with resistance to claims as a consequence.

While the American owner corporation cannot afford to ignore local management's opinions on insurance, it must consider the possibility that the opinions are ill informed. In its desire to minimize insurance costs and its belief that blue-collar employees cannot steal property of much value, management may scoff at the owner's opinion that a high-limit fidelity bond should apply to employees of all categories. If the owner defers to local management, permitting it to insure against embezzlement by only the comparatively few employees who make purchases, process receipts, prepare payrolls, write checks, or prepare computer programs, the affiliate may have to absorb much collaborative theft by employees of other categories.

A corporate director of risk control who does not weigh his own judgment against affiliates' opinions as to necessary amounts and breadth of insurance, therefore, is negligent.

Conditions Contributing to Superior Programs

In affiliates wholly owned by American corporations

Ideally, wholly owned affiliates secure their basic insurance covers in their countries' insurance markets. They thereby comply with laws requiring use of domestic brokers and insurers and earn the goodwill of the domestic brokers and insurers with which they do business. Increasingly, American-owned companies need the friendship of domestic businessmen to offset antagonism of politicians, journalists, and others.

Ideally too, affiliates do not try to force changes in attitudes in their domestic markets as to appropriate amounts of insurance and policy forms; they do not demand policy limits much higher than the insurers are accustomed to write or policy forms designed to meet conditions in the United States. Insurers which are unable to meet such demands are frustrated and view them as repudiation of domestic practices by arrogant Americans. Eventually, the resentment spreads outside the markets.

Behind the superiority of some insurance programs are overseas branches and associations of insurance companies based in the United States. These insurers have been licensed to sell in the markets of many countries. In most Latin American countries, moreover, they are registered as domestic companies, with majorities of their shares of stock owned by nationals. Established mainly to insure American operations in other countries, they are familiar with American views of insurance needs. Consequently, unless barred by law, they are prepared to provide whatever policy limits and forms are requested and to write policies in English, thus facilitating consistency in insuring at home and abroad.

American owner corporations do not, however, automatically require their foreign affiliates to insure with these extensions of American insurance companies. Price differences and the necessity of yielding to nationalism often cause them to employ nationals' insurance companies. Commonly, such patronage results in protection short of the owners' standards. To compensate for this lack the American owner possesses supplementary protection in the form of "worldwide" policies. Written, ordinarily, in the United States or London, such a policy greatly increases the amount of a particular kind of insurance applicable to a corporation's foreign affiliates. A "worldwide" liability policy, for example, might add $15 million of protection in countries where domestic insurers offer no more than the equivalent of $50,000.

Other excess policies cover perils excluded by domestic insurers. Much used for this purpose is Difference in Conditions insurance, a plan which expands property damage protection from coverage of a few itemized perils under a basic policy to "all risks" insurance. Because it supplements basic policies purchased in the domestic market, its use violates neither the letter nor the intent of laws requiring purchase of basic protection in affiliates' countries.

In affiliates owned partially by American corporations

The few insurance programs of jointly owned foreign affiliates which could be rated "superior" rest upon foundations like those underlying superior programs of American owner corporations. Atypical affiliates employ analytical and experienced insurance administrators whom they hold accountable and equip with authority. Contributing to the quality of some programs are those insurance administrators who are sufficiently self-confident to call upon the American owners' directors of risk control for information and advice. Unfortunately, many administrators fear that seeking such help reveals ignorance or lack of resourcefulness.

In the situation of a jointly owned affiliate employing no one with much knowledge of insurance, the condition most likely to produce a superior insurance program is close guidance by the American owner. With the American director of risk control authorized to prescribe the basic and excess policies, with the affiliate's management assisting by reporting changes in hazards, and with a skillful broker providing advice on use of the market in the affiliate's country, the owner corporation's investment will be admirably protected.

When control of insurance rests with domestic owners, superior programs may occur if the owners employ insurance administrators who are knowledgeable, have time to search for hazards, and are free to choose insurers on merit. As managers overseas adopt the view that risk control is a managerial function, American owner corporations will become increasingly confident that the overseas co-owners of their affiliates will insure effectively.

Ideally, from the standpoint of the American owner, a jointly owned company which is inadequately insured under policies secured in its domestic market has supplementary protection under the American corporation's "world-wide" policy. However, if such a corporation shares ownership of affiliates with companies in numerous countries, it might be forbidden by law to apply "world-wide" coverage to several affiliates. Under such restriction, superior insurance programs include supplementary covers which the affiliates secured individually. If the affiliates' domestic markets offer excess policies or if the affiliates are free to buy excess protection in London or other liberal markets, their protection could be entirely satisfactory to the American owner.

Systematic Loss Absorption

Of the three forms of risk control, only insurance is extensively used outside the United States and Canada. As indicated above, the prevailing attitude elsewhere toward casualty prevention is indifference. As indicated below, the common attitude abroad toward systematic absorption of casualty losses is one of skepticism. Because of insurance inadequacies, recovery of only portions of losses is commonplace. While such loss bearing does not qualify as "systematic," managers abroad who have been bitterly criticized for buying inadequate insurance have no interest in committing their companies to bearing losses intentionally.

Methods of Systematic Loss Absorption

The term "systematic loss absorption" here refers to three types of plans, some of which have been in widespread use for almost fifty years. One is the retention of revenues in order to cover losses in the future. Indicating the retentions are reserves in financial statements specifying the amounts retained and the kinds of losses to be absorbed. In some cases, the reserve accounts are backed by funds held solely for bearing losses. Under nonfunded plans, no such earmarking of assets occurs, although revenues in the amounts of the reserves have been kept in the companies. In event of loss, management extracts money from cash accounts and, if necessary, from whatever other forms of assets can be quickly liquidated. Ideally, highly liquid assets will be readily available in the amount of the loss.

Neither the funded nor the unfunded plan is much used now in the United States or elsewhere. The funded version is regarded as wasteful because the assets in the fund earn low interest rates. The nonfunded plan is criticized for the inherent uncertainty as to whether cash will be available in event of a large loss. Neither, therefore, will be examined further here.

Under another approach, the company merely expenses its casualties. Thus it treats casualty losses as operating costs to be borne out of current revenues. Some who use this method bear the full amounts of losses from accidents, burglaries, vandalism, embezzlement, or other designated perils during given periods of time. Most, however, absorb losses under deductibles clauses of policies, recovering from insurers the amounts of loss in excess of the deductibles. Other companies, under a similar plan, employ excess policies which establish ceilings upon the insured firms' exposures to losses, holding insurers liable for losses beyond the limits. Thus, a company plans to make workmen's compensation payments during a year up to a limit of $450,000. Thereafter, an insurance company would pay whatever additional amounts were necessary up to a maximum such as $4 million. Ordinarily, the aggregate amount to be absorbed before the excess insurer must participate is considerably larger than the portion of each loss to be borne under a policy deductible provision. Since the mid-sixties, however, deductible amounts such as $300,000 per loss have been used in property damage policies.

The most complex of the three approaches to systematic loss absorption is maintenance by large corporations of insurance subsidiaries for the purpose of insuring their units.[6] One such captive insurer has provided its parent company's operating units with liability and workmen's compensation insurance since 1911.[7] The great majority of them, however, have been established since 1960. With approximately 1,000 captives being operated by United States-based corporations by the late seventies, many in management clearly were reacting to the observation that the large corporation ultimately bears its own losses—paying premiums, over a few decades, approximately equal to its aggregate of losses. Under the captive plan, the parent company absorbs its losses currently via a facility capitalized to do so and takes down all or almost all of the investment income generated by the capital.

Most of the owners of captive insurers are based in the United States. However, the approach has an international aspect, for most of the captives are domiciled in Bermuda and other locations outside the United States.

With a captive insurance company employing a staff of insurance administrators and doing business at arm's length—more or less— with the parent company's other units, it differs greatly from the simple expensing of losses. Nevertheless, the assets of a captive are owned by the parent and its profits or losses are, finally, those of the parent.[8] The approach, therefore, qualifies as an elaborate form of systematic loss absorption.

Distaste Abroad for Systematic Loss Absorption

Whether or not a company abroad is an affiliate of an American corporation, its management probably has no interest in experimenting with any of the forms of loss absorption. The attitude stems partly from simple abhorrence of absorbing any portions of losses when insurers are available for bearing losses in full. In most countries, it is due also to lack of income tax incentives. Whereas the United States government bears 48 percent of a corporation's absorbed casualty loss (if the company has earned a net profit), the lower income tax rates of other countries preclude transfer of large portions of losses to the governments. Illustrative is the list of income tax rates below.

Country	Corporate Income Tax Rate (Percentages)
Argentina	33
Australia	37–50
Brazil	31–42
Denmark	36
France	50
Germany	15 if income distributed; 50 otherwise
Japan	26.7 if income distributed; 36.75 otherwise

Mexico	5–42 depending on amount of earnings
Netherlands	43–58 depending on amount of earnings
Norway	26.5
Philippines	25–35 depending on amount of earnings
Spain	30
Sweden	50 (approximate)
United Kingdom	40
Venezuela	60 on exploitive operations; 15–50 otherwise

Another deterrent, where insurers are willing to write deductibles, has been a combination of premium rate credits much too low to interest managers and failure of the managers to recognize the substantial long-term savings in administrative costs available by forgoing recoveries of large numbers of small losses. As companies throughout the world hire bona fide directors of risk control, overlooking such a potential for saving will occur less frequently.

In many countries in which insurance premium rates are established under tariffs (i.e., compacts or laws requiring all insurers to charge standard premium rates), opposition to deductibles has been powerful. Application of standard rates to policies including varied deductibles is difficult, if not impossible. With many insurers and many governments favoring the orderliness of noncompetitive pricing under tariffs, this barrier to use of deductibles will not be lifted in the near future.

A condition in some countries which might bar the use of loss absorption plans forever is dependence of national governments upon premium taxes. Governments in all countries are fond of premium taxation. They appreciate the minimal costs of collection and the absence of taxpayers' resentment. (Few policyholders are aware of such taxes or the fact that they are the ultimate bearers thereof.) If, moreover, a government collects premium taxes equal to as much as 40 percent of insurers' premium income, it does not applaud plans to use deductibles or any other means of premium reduction.

Decision Making as to Expensing Losses

To American corporations which cannot force their wholly owned or partly owned affiliates to use deductibles clauses or excess policies over large loss absorption limits, the merits of such risk bearing are irrelevant. Many owner corporations, however, are free of such constraints and must therefore decide whether they should direct their affiliates to employ loss absorption plans. As in deciding whether to bear losses out of pocket in the United States, they begin by ascertaining whether the plans would afford savings with certainty. If so, they must, of course, implement the plans.[9] If not, loss absorption would be speculative, and corporate policy on speculation indicates the affiliates' course of action.

Decision Making as to Use of Captive Insurers

American corporations which control the insurance programs of their foreign affiliates have little difficulty in deciding whether to require the affiliates to insure with captive insurers. If the affiliates are legally able to insure in that manner and clearly would save substantially, they should employ captives. An exception to this generality would stem from the necessity to insure commercially for a tactical reason, for example, when a very important customer which owns an insurance company demands reciprocity.

Owners of affiliates in countries which require purchase of basic covers in domestic markets likewise are not in doubt: their captives are not domiciled in the affiliates' countries and therefore cannot insure the affiliates unless they differ from almost all other captives by selling excess covers.

Evaluating Performance in Risk Control

As indicated in Chapter 1, top management is responsible for appraising performance in risk control. Mentioned as a barrier to exact evaluation is the impossibility of quantifying the results of casualty prevention programs. Another barrier is the futility of comparing insurance expenditures of one company with those of another; differences in hazards, insurable values, and breadth of protection necessitate wide differences in cost. Still another difficulty is the fact that management learns whether or not its insurance programs are adequate only if the company incurs a major casualty.

In addition to these universal difficulties in evaluating, problems develop out of the various relationships between owner corporations and their foreign affiliates. The sections below outline some of these problems.

Jointly Owned Companies Directed by Overseas Owners

Although an American corporation may be barred from advising its foreign affiliates in risk control, it must protect its stockholders by keeping apprised of the effectiveness of the affiliates' programs. If its surveillance reveals that an affiliate incurred an operating loss because insurance protection fell $2 million short of losses in two embezzlements or that an affiliate retreated from proposed expansion in the baseless fear that it could not cope economically with risks of loss through casualties, the owner corporation must gain the right to participate in risk control or terminate its investment in the affiliate.

While evaluation of the affiliate's risk control is the responsibility of the owner's top management, it ordinarily is performed by the corporate director of risk control. He bases his conclusions on his critical study of the reports of the domestic owner or the affiliate and, sometimes, on analyses by insurance brokers.

Affiliates under Control of American Owner

Ideally, top management of a corporation which closely supervises risk control in its foreign affiliate evaluates performance at home and abroad in the same manner. It begins by reviewing data on absorbed losses and expenditures for insurance and prevention in terms of the corporation's primary and secondary risk control purposes. Concurrently, it examines periodic reports of the director of risk control on changes in the affiliate's risk control programs, on the reasons behind them, and on defects in the programs caused by constraints imposed by top management. The key to a successful review is management's ability to weigh accurately the validity of the reasoning underlying the statements of the risk controllers.

A second step begins with top management's study of opinions of the affiliate's managers as to strengths and weaknesses of its programs. After that management studies the comments of the corporate director of risk control on those opinions. If top management excels in separating realities from contentions based on ignorance, bias, misinformation, or mythology, it arrives finally at reasonably accurate conclusions as to the effectiveness of the programs. At intervals of three or four years, it obtains corroboration or repudiation of its findings from brokers or other consultants. When its evaluation differs greatly from that of the outsider, it discusses the programs with the affiliate's managers and the corporate director of risk control. If the discussions were productive, management gains additional insights into the quality of their reasoning, and, perhaps, into their effectiveness.

Affiliates Controlling Their Systems of Risk Control

Whether an affiliate operating autonomously in risk control is owned entirely or in part by an American corporation, the purpose of risk control evaluation is to ascertain whether earnings are threatened or reduced significantly by ineptitude. Therefore, top management needs to learn only whether the affiliate's performance has been effective.

Again, it must weigh the statements of the corporate director of risk control, of management of the affiliate, and, occasionally, of consultants for quality of reasoning.

NOTES

1. The forms of casualties considered in this study are theft, extortion, legal liability, damage to facilities, death or disability of especially valuable employees, punitive and exploitive acts of governments, and inability to use facilities because of strikes, civil disorder, terrorist threats, or other coercive efforts.
2. Ordinarily, the broker provides such help in anticipation of commissions for placement of insurance, but he may also work on the fee basis.
3. In some cases, however, the data rest upon myths. Whereas generations of managers may have believed that employees in their country rarely steal from their employers, large amounts of loss through employee theft may be attributed erroneously each year to shoplifting and faulty record keeping.
4. A trend toward awarding more attractive rate reductions for the use of sprinkler systems was apparent by the opening of the seventies: insurers in some countries have reduced fire rates by 50 percent on installations which have them.
5. American owner corporations are more commonly barred from control of affiliates' insurance programs than from control of casualty prevention.
6. By the mid-seventies a trend toward opening the facilities of captives to companies unrelated to the parent companies had become apparent.
7. General Electric Corporation established its Electric Mutual Insurance Company in that year in hope of reducing insurance costs.
8. Increasingly, in the United States, captives serve several owners. Some have been formed collaboratively; others were organized by single corporations which later sold interests to several other companies.
9. Two sets of circumstances constitute opportunities for assured savings through deductibles or excess plans. One rests upon ability to predict the minimum amount of loss which will develop out of an area of risk in a specified period of time. If management knows that theft by employees could amount to the equivalent of $8 million in a year and will amount to at least $500,000, the company can save money with certainty by absorbing that predictable minimum each year *if the insurer will respond by reducing the annual premium by (1) the $500,000 of loss to be absorbed and (2) the amount it would have spent otherwise in processing the losses making up that inevitable minimum.* The net savings will equal the amount that the insurer would have charged for its processing of the first $500,000 in losses.

   The other opportunity for assured savings stems from ability to predict the minimum cost of effecting a recovery under a policy. Illustrative is the situation of a corporation which cannot recover a loss of any amount without spending at least $400 (in terms of time spent in filing the claim, discussing it with the insurer, and recording and depositing the payment). To recover less than $400, therefore, would be wasteful, and the company should absorb each such loss. The savings will equal the rate credit awarded by the insurer and whatever portions of $400 are saved by not filing claims for losses of less than that amount.

3

TRENDS IN THE PERIL OF LEGAL
LIABILITY ABROAD

Two aspects of the peril of legal liability for damage to human bodies, property, or reputations are especially significant. One is that in no other country is the peril nearly so menacing as in the United States. The other, however, is that in virtually all other countries it is becoming greater.

Indicative of the difference between the liability climate in the United States and that in any other country is the difference in the number of suits for damages brought against manufacturers whose products are alleged to have caused bodily injuries or damage to property. In the United States, the peril of products liability has assumed nightmarish proportions: companies of all sizes regularly contend with claimants, and the insurance market struggles to meet demands for high levels of protection. Conversely, in Argentina, Brazil, Chile, Denmark, Italy, Mexico, Norway, Spain, Sweden, and Venezuela, claims for damages based upon allegedly faulty products are rare. And in Australia, Belgium, France, Germany, the Netherlands, and the United Kingdom, products claims have become a matter of some concern—mainly to producers of foods and other consumables—only during the past half-dozen years.[1]

Similarly, whereas liability for the gradual infliction of harm could be so costly in the United States that insurers have revised liability policies to cover such happenings, in no other country do corporations worry about it. Even in Germany and the United Kingdom, where enthusiasm for suing is rising, observers are confident that courts would refuse to award full damages to persons claiming that they had been made sick, for example, by prolonged exposure to noxious fumes. The courts feel, apparently, that one who experiences symptoms of bodily injury from a known cause and makes no effort to avoid further damage is partly at fault.

Another aspect of the legal liability climate in the United States which sets it apart from those of other countries is the common practice of filing nuisance claims. Encouraged by the knowledge that many companies dispose of claims whigh are either spurious or barely valid by settling out of court for small fractions of the amounts sought, many thousands of persons in the United States file such claims as an avocation. British companies are similarly annoyed but to a much lesser degree. Elsewhere, nuisance claims occur rarely. Moreover, professional "accident" victims are rareties outside the United States. Indeed, in most countries even many persons in the insurance business have never encountered such frauds.

While risk of liability loss to industrial and commercial companies is still a much less costly problem in all other countries than in it is the United States, during the past decade it has moved from insignificance to varying degrees of menace. The escalation has been very slight in Scandinavia, Italy, Spain, and the Latin American countries other than Venezuela, but elsewhere it now is regarded as formidable. In particular, awards have soared in Australia, Germany, and the United Kingdom.

Conditions Underlying Legal Liability

The likelihood that a United States-based corporation conducting operations abroad will suffer heavy losses in consequence of accidental damage to bodies, properties, or reputations depends only in part upon the care with which its employees perform their duties. Beyond the control of the company is the country's legal liability climate, that combination of statutes, court decisions, attitudes, and practices which establishes the probabilities that companies will have to compensate claimants. This chapter is a survey of prospects of corporate liability losses outside the United States.

The Statutes

Statutes in some countries are such formidable barriers to winning in court that accident victims are deterred from suing for damages. Those in other countries encourage seeking such redress. In general, as indicated in the sections "Negligence Under Codified Systems of Law" and "Courts' Views of Negligence," plaintiffs are less likely to win damages in the countries where codes closely control the decisions made by the courts than in countries in which the courts are not thus restricted. Deterrence to filing for damages also results from statutory limits upon amounts to be recovered by claimants. In a few countries statutory ceilings are so low that they discourage all but the most determined and affluent of accident victims from suing.

Also contributing in some countries to the disinclination to seek damages are the combined influences of social security statutes and courts' attitudes. If a country's social security statutes provide comprehensive medical and income-replacement benefits and its courts are reluctant to award liberally for pain or other suffering, few victims of bodily injuries are likely to sue. Denmark, Italy, and Sweden are foremost among the countries in which such a combination of influences prevail. Thus, the Swedish parents of a child who has lost several fingers accept the state's complete medical care and, aware of the virtual certainty that a court would award nothing for the child's pain or their anxiety, take no legal action against the negligent driver who caused the accident.

The most common type of statute tending to increase the incidence of damages suits is that requiring maintenance of insurance for the protection of persons who might be injured by the policyholders. Such a law is likely to be especially influential in countries in which the populace heretofore has had no inclination to sue. In Spain, for example, a relatively new compulsory auto compensation insurance law probably is publicizing the economic opportunities available via lawsuits. While auto accident victims need not sue in order to recover under the law, the new opportunities to recover sizeable sums following accidents may lead shortly to widespread suing in consequence of nonautomotive accidents. Similarly, as Mexico's social security system is extended to areas of the country not now covered, millions of Mexicans who have become accustomed to the bearing of their costs of job-related injuries by others will be conditioned to seek recoveries from the causers of accidents which are unrelated to their occupations.

An example of a form of statutory encouragement to seek recovery for damage to property through the courts is a French law which holds contractors and architects responsible for collapse of buildings within ten years of completion of construction. Under recent liberal interpretations of that statute, French building owners regularly recover the costs of repairing cracks in plaster and paint and otherwise are inspired to search for ways to thrust costs of building repairs or maintenance upon other persons.

The Courts

An important element of the climate of legal liability in any country is the nature of the courts which hear tort cases. In countries in which liability suits are tried before laymen, arguments are geared to feelings of sympathy, resentment, horror, or prejudice. Although judges provide jurors with definitions of the law as it applies to the cases they are hearing and sometimes caution them against making their decisions on the basis of emotion, jurors ordinarily are more likely than judges to permit emotion to affect their findings both as to where liability rests and as to values of damages. Indicative thereof are the many instances each year of reversals of juries' decisions and reductions in juries' awards for damages.

Except in the United States and the United Kingdom, jury trials of tort cases are almost unknown, and even in British trial courts, judges, rather than juries, set the amounts of awards.

Practices of Lawyers

Lawyers' modes of operation have significant influence on climates of legal liability. The manner in which a lawyer becomes the representative of the accident victim is one such mode. Another is the way he obtains his fee. The methods vary considerably from country to country.

Soliciting accident victims

Presumably, in seeking out accident victims to induce them to sue, lawyers cause the filing of suits which could not have occurred otherwise. Codes of ethics in all countries forbid lawyers to solicit business in this manner. That prohibition, however, is more real in some countries than in others. Such solicitation usually is performed surreptitiously and close comparisons of the extent of its use are therefore impossible. However, some insurance executives feel that the practice is more common in France, the United States, and Venezuela than elsewhere. In France and Venezuela and most of the other European countries it seems to have become increasingly common since the mid-fifties.

While ambulance chasing is not likely in the near future to become so common anywhere as to greatly increase numbers of suits for damages, a German observer has predicted that the practice will become increasingly common in all countries of northern Europe because larger numbers of young persons are being educated. As more and more persons move into the professions, he believes, the growing supply of young lawyers will necessitate an increasingly aggressive search for clients.

Contingent fee system

In the United States, lawyers ordinarily contract to represent accident victims in return for specified percentages (usually in the 25–50 percent range) of whatever sums are awarded by the courts or are obtained through settlements out of court (the contingent fee system). Under such an arrangement, a person who has been injured in an accident sues even though he lacks funds for paying lawyers. If the plan is not available, an accident victim of modest means usually decides against taking the chance of having to pay a lawyer with his own funds in the event he loses in court.

The contingent fee system is very little used outside the United States. In some countries it is prohibited by statutes.[2] In most, however, it is barred either by custom or by codes of ethics. In no country employing such restrictions, seemingly, is the contingent fee likely to become permissible in the near future.

The only significant exceptions to the general distaste for the system outside the United States are the situations in Germany and Italy. Italian lawyers are essentially free to bargain for percents of the proceeds of suits but are limited by statute to a maximum of 25 percent. German lawyers charge on the basis of statutory schedules of percentages of clients' recoveries, commonly receiving 20 percent. Observers in the two countries feel that those controlled contingent fee plans have not caused appreciable rises in award levels. While some expect such an effect eventually, few predict substantial increases.

Dissemination of News

A very important factor in the increasing incidence of suing for damages has been the publicizing—by the press, in particular—of spectacular court awards and settlements in the United States and elsewhere.[3] While lawyers and insurance executives everywhere have long been aware of the workings of the legal liability system in the United States, only since the mid-fifties have newspapers and popular periodicals brought word to the public of sensational awards for damages. Enlivening this process of education has been the emotional and biased reporting which long has been a part of journalism in many countries. Throughout the world, consequently, persons who would not have considered suing under any circumstances a few years ago now daydream of windfall recoveries after incurring painless sprains and bruises.

Bases of Liability for Damages

The legal systems of all countries provide for imposition of legal liability on several bases. The first section below describes patterns of law under which persons become liable for the consequences of their negligence. Subsequent sections treat of three sets of circumstances under which persons are held liable in tort on bases other than negligence.

Conditions and Developments Underlying Negligence Law

Negligence law in any country derives from attitudes and opinions of legislators, jurists, lawyers, and, indeed, of common citizens. An understanding of the present status of a country's negligence system, therefore, requires a knowledge of the attitudes and opinions which have shaped the system. Likewise, the ability to anticipate the future shape of such a system requires awareness of trends in attitudes and opinions.

Philosophical background

Behind all systems of negligence law are a few philosophical positions. The most basic is the belief that no body of law can long survive unless it is rooted in morality. In the view of the Stoics of early Greece, morality was simply an expression of reason, and reason was the essential law of the universe. The Romans adopted the philosophy, and as they moved through the centuries of building and governing their empire they convinced others of its rationality. On the question of legal responsibilities for negligent behavior, the moralistic principle held as follows: "Any human act which causes damage to another person obliges that person through whose fault it has occurred to repair it."[4] Thus, belief in responsibility is reflected in such descendants of Roman civil law as the legal systems of France, Italy, Spain, Belgium, Greece, Switzerland, Germany, Austria, Latin America, Turkey, and Japan. It also has been incorporated into legal systems which do not reflect many other Roman concepts. Principal systems of this latter category are those of the Scandinavian nations, Britain, Canada, Australia, and the United States.

Although almost all countries in which American companies conduct substantial operations observe the fault-indemnity rule, the patterns of observance differ. Thus, the French regard the principle with such passion that they sue for damages much more frequently than citizens of any other European country. Sometimes they sue for amounts so small as to make the suits economically pointless. To the Frenchman, apparently, the cause of justice requires that he seek redress in the law for any degree of financial harm at the negligent hands of another. In Latin America, conversely, suits for damages are filed—with rare exceptions—only by businessmen and professional persons. Rank-and-file Latin Americans seem less moved by consciousness of responsibility for negligent behavior than by a submissiveness to fate.

In the United Kingdom, the fault-indemnity principle applies in conjunction with the belief that the individual is obliged to exert reasonable efforts to ward off harm from negligent acts of others. Typically, a Briton who for several months has smelled gas each time he has used his new space heater but has made no effort to correct the condition will be inclined to feel that he has forfeited his right to sue the manufacturer or installer following a gas explosion. Unfortunately, for manufacturers of gas heaters and others, this aspect of the British sense of responsibility is probably beginning to fade.

In Denmark, the fault-indemnity principle is somewhat obscured by the prevailing belief that each person is his brother's keeper. Therefore a Dane tends to be reluctant to attempt to thrust the cost of his personal misfortunes upon others even when their negligence may have contributed to his accident. A Dane whose auto accident was due partly to his speeding and partly to a slightly defective steering system would be unlikely to attempt to recoup by suing the manufacturer.

A second philosophical view common to almost all the countries in which American-based companies do business is the concept of the law as a system which is endlessly adaptive. With respect to the fixing of responsibility for losses due to negligence, that concept makes possible the systematic finding of fault in the ever-changing circumstances of accidents spawned by social and economic change. In all countries lawmakers recognized that they could not define negligence so completely as to leave no questions of rights and responsibities in every future accident. Instead, they left to the courts the task of translating guidelines into findings in the unimaginable situations of the future.

Negligence under codified systems of law

In deciding whether or not defendants in suits for damages have been guilty of negligence, the nations are in two broad categories. In one, all law is stated in written codes and the task of the court is to resolve the question by applying relevant sections of the code. This approach was the essence of Roman civil law and is observed today throughout continental Europe (with the exception of Denmark and the Netherlands), in most nations of the Near East and North Africa, in all of Latin America, and in Japan and the Republic of the Philippines.

The other category includes those countries in which the particular court applies "to the cause in hand the judicial experience of the past rather than trying to fit the cause into its exact logical (and codified) pigeonhole. . . ."[5] The principal exponents of this method are the common law countries, i.e., the United Kingdom, the United States, Canada, and Australia. The Scandinavian states, the Netherlands, South Africa, and India ordinarily are not classified as either "common law" or "civil law" states.[6] In treating negligence questions, however, the courts of the Scandinavian countries and the Netherlands rely more frequently upon codified guidance than upon opinions of courts in earlier cases, while Indian and South African courts must look only to judicial precedents.

Among the countries relying substantially upon codified descriptions of negligent behavior, wide differences exist in the scrupulousness with which the courts perform their duty to resolve questions in terms of provisions in the codes. French courts have not regarded the Napoleonic Codes with much seriousness for many years, seeking guidance in decisions of other courts almost as routinely as do British courts. In Mexico, Venezuela, Brazil, and Argentina, conversely, the courts rarely seek guidance beyond the codes. German courts occupy a middle position on this score. In the large majority of cases, they struggle dutifully to employ codified provisions reflecting nineteenth century social and economic conditions. Quite frequently, however, they study commercial and industrial usages in order to ascertain whether customary standards of care had been observed by the persons charged with negligence. Also, since an overriding provision of the code requires that the parties to any business transaction act in good faith, in cases involving business dealings they sometimes look to the thoughts of other courts on the nature of performance in good faith.

Absence of definitions of negligence

In all countries which rely substantially upon provisions of written codes in deciding cases of alleged negligence the codes lack references to certain concepts which, in the United States, constitute access routes to finding negligence. These concepts, described below, have been a very important factor in the magnitude of the legal liability peril in the United States, for they tend to make persons and corporations vulnerable to damages claims. In those countries in which these concepts do not apply, because the courts continue to rely heavily upon codes, legal liability remains a remote threat. Conversely, in countries in which the courts increasingly look beyond codes in settling negligence questions, the courts probably will emulate those of the United States by recognizing the concepts as valid and will thereby raise the likelihood of loss via liability. Such emulation, however, probably will develop slowly. In none of the countries in which case law is paramount have the courts adopted all the concepts.

The attractive nuisance rule is a product of pressure since World War II to transfer responsibility for physical and economic well-being from the weak to the strong. It prescribes an exceedingly high standard of care on the part of property owners to protect children against injuries resulting from their impetuous trespassing upon intriguing items of property. Conceivably, the casual regard of French jurists for the restrictiveness of the civil code and a widespread protective attitude could produce awards of the attractive nuisance type in France during the next few years. In Italy the combination of some willingness in the courts to move outside the confines of the code under extenuating circumstances and of a spirit of paternalism which has lingered in some courts since the Fascist era increases the possibility of such decisions in the immediate future. Otherwise, adoption overseas of the attractive nuisance concept is most unlikely for at least the next decade.

Also included in no code is the dangerous instrumentality rule. In the United States, a court which has agreed with the contention of an accident victim that the manufactured item which inflicted his injury should be designated a "dangerous instrumentality" thereupon holds the defendant manufacturer responsible for his product to a level which is second only to an absolute guarantee of safety. The court also bars use by the manufacturer of the defense of privity of contract, under which an accident victim can recover from the manufacturer only if he had been the purchaser of the injurious item. Thus, in the United States dangerous instrumentality has added greatly to the difficulty of defending against negligence claims. However, its incorporation into any civil code seems unlikely in the foreseeable future.

Still another facet of the negligence concept in the United States which has no counterpart in any civil code is that of *res ipsa loquitur.* When a court agrees with the plaintiff's contention that *res ipsa loquitur* applies, the burden of proof shifts, in effect, to the defendant. The defendant, that is, must prove that he has not negligently caused the plaintiff's injury. Ordinarily, a court invokes *res ipsa loquitur* after the plaintiff has demonstrated that (a) the accident cannot be accounted for in terms of negligence on the plaintiff's part, (b) the defendant was the only person who could have so prepared or so used the article which caused the injury as to make the mishap possible, and (c) the article could not have caused the injury unless negligence had occurred in its manufacture, use, or maintenance. Clearly, the availability of *res ipsa loquitur* is of great value to the plaintiff who might have difficulty in proving the defendant's negligence under the broad standard of failure to exercise reasonable care under whatever circumstances.

The concept of *res ipsa loquitur* is almost unknown in countries employing codes and is not likely to become a part of negligence law in the foreseeable future. However, a few codes include the concept's burden-of-proof feature to a limited extent. Notable is the Spanish code, which provides that the defendant in an auto accident suit can avoid liability only by proving that the plaintiff's negligence was the sole cause of the accident. Greater difficulty, therefore, must be anticipated in defending against claims developing from auto accidents in Spain than in other civil code countries.

Harsh codified definitions of negligence

In a few instances, civil codes prescibe standards of behavior which are more severe, from the standpoint of the prospective defendant, than those applicable throughout the United States. The codes of Belgium, Germany, and France hold owners of property adjoining sidewalks responsible for the condition of the walks. If, therefore, a passerby were injured in a fall upon a slippery sidewalk in Belgium, the owner would be liable for damages if he had failed to exercise reasonably effective means to remove the ice within a reasonable period after it had formed. In the United States, according to the majority of decisions in such cases, the municipality, not the private property owner, is responsible for keeping the walks free of hazards.[7] Only if he has negligently caused a flow of water which froze on the walk or, in attempting to remove ice or snow, has made travel even more dangerous is the property owner likely to be adjudged guilty of negligent maintenance.

Another prescription under the French code which exceeds in severity the findings of courts in the United States is the liability of the tenant to his landlord for damage to the premises. Under the provision, the court presumes negligence of the tenant in the event of damage from fire or from virtually any other cause. In the United States, unless the lease holds the tenant responsible for damage without regard to cause, the courts require tenants to indemnify owners only if they have been proven guilty of negligence.

The Mexican code provides for payment of punitive damages equal to one-third of the amount of actual damage by defendants who have been found guilty of gross negligence. In the United States, punitive damages ordinarily are awarded in situations in which the actual damages are minimal because good luck alone saved the defendants' outrageously negligent behavior from causing severe injuries or extensive property damage. Mexican courts, however, rarely deal with the concept of gross negligence and have awarded punitive damages in very few cases. If, however, the number of damages claims filed in Mexican courts increases as substantially as predicted by some observers, punitive awards can be expected to become much more common.

The most important of the codified arrangements to undermine the position of the defendant is the comparative negligence rule. Although a slow trend toward a version of this ancient principle is under way in the United States,[8] the courts of most states still enforce the contributory negligence rule, under which the plaintiff is unable to recover if even a slight degree of negligence on his part contributed to the occurrence of the accident. Under the comparative negligence system specified in the civil codes, however, in the event that both parties are guilty of apparent negligence the court attempts to ascertain the extent of the negligence of each. If it concludes that the plaintiff's negligence was slight and the defendant's negligence gross, it awards damages equal to the full amount of the plaintiff's loss. Theoretically, then, defendants are more likely to be required to pay under comparative negligence than under contributory negligence.

However, the fact that the comparative negligence rule is prescribed in almost all civil codes does not necessarily mean that U.S. companies operating internationally will be more threatened by liability abroad than at home. A countervailing factor is the common practice of the courts to observe the contributory negligence rule to temper the severity of the rule in cases of painful and costly injuries. Thus, if negligence on the part of a grievously injured plaintiff had contributed to only a trivial degree to the occurrence of the accident, the court is likely to award damages in almost the amount it would have fixed had the defendant alone been negligent. In practice, then, the contributory negligence system functions much as the comparative negligence system of the civil code countries. Moreover, the form of comparative negligence rule which has gained a foothold in the United States places the defendant at a considerably greater disadvantage than it would have experienced under the older version. It requires the court to measure both the negligence of the plaintiff and the negligence of the defendant in order to apportion the costs accordingly. Thus, if the defendant's negligence had been valued at 40 percent of the total and the plaintiff's at 60 percent, the award to the plaintiff would represent 40 percent of the court's estimate of his losses. Under this version of the rule, a plaintiff whose negligence was a relatively minor factor in the occurrence of an accident would be required to contribute commensurately to the bearing of the loss, while it would have had to pay nothing in a civil code country.

Courts' views of negligence

Whether obliged to enforce civil codes or not, the courts of all countries test for negligence by attempting, essentially, to ascertain whether or not the defendants have behaved with the same regard for the bodies or property of the plaintiffs that they would have exercised toward their own. However, distinct differences exist in the pursuit of that objective. In some countries the courts view the claims of all persons alleging injury through the negligence of others with deep skepticism. They anticipate that the evidence will indicate that the plaintiffs filed their claims erroneously or speculatively. Few claimants are able to dispel such suspicion.[9] Countries in this category are Argentina, Brazil, Denmark, Germany, Mexico, the Netherlands, Spain, and Sweden.

In another category are countries in which the courts are dedicated to upholding the fault system but are sympathetic toward the claims of accident victims. In the United Kingdom, for example, they sternly reject claims which are not clearly grounded on defendants' failure to exercise reasonable care, but they observe the concept of comparative negligence. They also have established a counterpart to the attractive nuisance doctrine by finding property owners liable for negligence in some cases of injury to trespassers who were too young to recognize danger.

The courts in some countries of this category can be expected eventually to invoke the *res ipsa loquitur* rule. However, few, if any, decisions clearly resting upon that rule had been handed down during the seventies.

A third group consists of countries in which some courts attempt to relieve situations of proverty through their rulings in negligence cases. In a case in which the evidence has not shown conclusively that the defendant was or was not negligent, such a court finds a highly solvent defendant liable for negligence in order to save the crippled plaintiff from economic disaster. Likewise, a court thus motivated tends to ignore applicable statutory or case law which it regards as illogical, observing instead its own more humane standards. Observers of the judiciary in Belgium, Brazil, Denmark, France, and Norway feel that this ameliorative attitude accounts for numerous findings of negligence in their countries.

Differences in the courts' attitudes toward persons attributing illness or wounds to injurious products is another basis of classifying countries. In no other country do the courts rule as sympathetically toward victims of alleged negligence in the manufacturing or distributing of products as in the United States. The situation can be likened to a game of follow-the-leader, in which the United States is trailed by groups of countries. The closest followers seem to be Belgium, France, the Netherlands, and the United Kingdom. In those countries the courts consistently hold manufacturers and distributors to high standards of care.[10] As indicated below, they also are beginning to emulate courts in the United States by permitting claimants to recover via routes less laborious than that of proving negligence. Trailing by a greater distance is another cluster consisting of Germany, Norway, Sweden, and Venezuela. In each of those countries the courts are not adverse to hearing products claims, but they seldom hold manufacturers or distributors responsible for injuries to users of their products. Bringing up the rear are the many other countries where the courts view products suits against manufacturers or marketers so suspiciously that very few persons undertake such actions. In those countries the courts probably will move gradually toward holding manufacturers and distributors to increasingly high standards of care.

Conditions and Developments Underlying Strict Liability

The most significant recent change in the liability peril to corporations in the United States has been the courts' acceptance of the principle of strict liability. Under this principle, a court may find a company liable for damages without giving any consideration to the question of negligence. Insofar as manufacturers are concerned, the core of strict liability is the implied warranty that the product can be used without injurious effects. In its harshest version in the United States, it manifests the "deep-pocket" view of the manner in which costs arising out of bodily injuries or property damage should be borne. The law, that is, regards the manufacturer as better fitted than the customer to bear the costs of an injury involving its product. Furthermore, as courts and legislatures move to place the consumer virtually beyond blame in such an incident, they ignore the possibility that he might have contributed substantially to the occurrence of the accident.

In its less tilted form, strict liability does not hold the manufacturer responsible if alteration of the product by the victim or a third party had been the cause of the accident. By the beginning of the seventies, strict liability had supplanted negligence as the most common basis of demands by persons claiming to have been harmed by manufacturers' products.

Similarly, utilities companies face the prospect that in most suits resulting from accidents involving such facilities as transmission lines, transformer stations, and pipelines they will not be charged with negligence. Instead, the claimants will ask that the companies be held liable simply because their property damaged bodies or property.

Imposing legal liability without evidence of fault is not an American innovation: England's Codes of Æthelberht of the seventh century held property owners automatically responsible if their property caused damage to the property of others. While the Codes were abandoned centuries ago, derivations survive in many countries in the form of workmen's compensation statutes. A less common descendant is the auto compensation law. Under such a statute, the owner (or driver, in some cases) of a car involved in an accident becomes liable—essentially without regard to fault—for injuries suffered by pedestrians or occupants of the other vehicle. Among countries having auto compensation statutes are Mexico, Spain, and Sweden.

Few strict liability statutes apply to accidents other than those involving autos. However, German statutes hold companies which pollute surface or ground water liable without consideration of fault and impose strict liability upon owners of gas and electric plants for whatever injuries they cause. Also, a French statute places strict liability upon users of nuclear energy in the production of electric power or of radioisotopes in industrial operations. By the mid-eighties, most of the other industrialized countries likewise will be employing such statutes for pollution control.

Except in those countries which either have already imposed strict liability by statutes or will do so in the future, the probability of a corporation's being held liable without evidence of fault in its operations outside the United States is low. The courts in civil code countries are not at all likely to hold defendants to the standard of strict liability if the circumstances of the accidents are not covered by strict liability statutes. An exception, conceivably, might be the French courts: some French lawyers and insurance men anticipate that illnesses or deaths relating to use of medicines will inspire "Cutter Laboratories decisions" in the courts even in absence of pertinent statutes.[11] Insofar as the courts of countries outside the civil code bloc are concerned, only those of Australia, Canada, Japan, Sweden, and the United Kingdom are likely to impose strict liability without statutory sanction. Swedish courts tend to find liability without fault in cases in which the defendants are engaged in heavy industry, transportation, or providing of power or fuel. Courts in the United Kingdom, Australia, and Canada have begun granting awards to victims of breaches of implied warranties. No indication exists that courts of many countries will follow such leads.

Calculating Amounts of Damages

The amounts of damages awarded outside the United States vary greatly from country to country. In no other country, however, do they approach the levels of damages awarded in the United States.

Statutory Limits on Awards

Although numerous countries have defined legal liability in codes, very few have prescribed statutory limits of liability for those who do harm to others. In absence of statutory ceilings, plaintiffs' awards are limited in amount only by the precedents established by other courts. Because court precedents are easier to replace than statutory provisions, award levels are more changeable in those countries in which codified limits do not apply.

Illustrative of the influence of statutory restriction is the situation in Denmark, where award levels have been geared—seemingly—to the low salaries of legislators and judges and have been unrealistically low in terms of costs of goods and services. Whereas an injured Dane cannot recover more than the statutory limit of the equivalent of $10,300, a similarly damaged Swede might be awarded the equivalent of $100,000 by a court which was not obliged to observe a fixed ceiling. And while, in due course, that Danish limit might be doubled by legislative action, precedents for awards equivalent to $250,000 or more might be established in Swedish courts.

Mexico's code provides for a maximum award for disability of the equivalent of about $3,300.[12] With Venezuelan courts guided only by precedence in such cases, severely disabled Venezuelans have recovered amounts exceeding the equivalent of $100,000. Mexicans predict that the statutory limit will rise from time to time, but legislators are not likely to be as responsive to pressures for higher awards as the Venezuelan courts.

Practices in the Courts

In countries which do not employ codified restraints upon liability awards, two developments in the courts indicate that management must expect the costs of legal liability to rise considerably in many countries. One is the attempting to indemnify the accident victim fully for his out-of-pocket costs. The other is over indemnification by awarding damages exceeding those costs.

Trend toward indemnification

Theoretically, indemnification always has been the guidemark employed in the setting of awards. In actuality, the courts of most countries have fully indemnified few victims of bodily injuries. They have based awards upon custom or other considerations of little relevance to the particular victim, or they have sought to achieve full indemnification only in the cases of wealthy or otherwise influential plaintiffs. Among countries other than the United States and Canada, the outstanding example of the movement toward full indemnification through court awards is Germany. German courts regularly examine closely such criteria of loss as the individual's present and prospective salary levels, his prospect of diminshed effectiveness on the job due to lingering disabilty, and his long-term medical costs. Therefore, a corporation which is responsible for having destroyed the career of a promising young German banker quite likely will be ordered to pay the equivalent of upwards of $100,000. British courts, too, are consistently awarding sums which closely reflect losses.

In nearly all countries in which codified limits do not restrict liability awards, the trend is under way to award those who incur bodily injuries or property damage the full values of their losses. Substantial rises in award levels seem inevitable in almost all countries during the next decade.

Basing of awards on other considerations

The extent to which courts look beyond accident victims' out-of-pocket costs in calculating damages largely determines the abruptness with which award levels rise. As the courts in other countries emulate those in the United States by (1) awarding punitive damages to victims of particularly irresponsible behavior, (2) weighing the capacities of the accident victims and those who caused their injuries for absorbing losses, and (3) granting compensation for mental and physical suffering, they raise their awards spectacularly.

Punitive damages

In awarding punitive damages, courts reject the theory that damages are paid only to repair financial wounds. Often, they grant such awards to persons who—largely by chance—escaped harm in near misses caused by the defendant's outrageous negligence. Until the early seventies, courts in the United States rarely awarded punitive damages in excess of a few thousand dollars. By the mid-seventies, however, courts which found defendants guilty of gross disregard for the well-being of the plaintiffs were awarding very large damages. Unless the liability peril is brought under control by legislation, ever larger punitive damages can be expected. In other countries, however, observers do not anticipate that the courts ever will legitimize the idea of the punishing via damages. At present, Mexico may be the only other country in which the courts regularly consider awarding punitive damages. Mexican courts, however, are bound by statute to limit the punitive damages to one-third the amount of the economic damages. Punitive awards in the United States typically exceed economic damages by many times.

Ability to pay

The fact that jurors and judges routinely consider the defendants' ability to pay damages is a major reason for the rise of awards levels over the past two decades in the United States. Ordinarily, large corporations and wealthy individuals are ordered to pay more than small companies and unskilled laborers. Courts gauge corporate capacity to pay in terms of profitability of operations and, increasingly, of protection under high limits of liability insurance.

In few other countries have prosperous companies had much reason to worry about such discrimination. However, ability-to-pay has taken root in France, Italy, Norway and, in particular, the Netherlands. While Dutch courts are not universally committed to the principle, many systematically consider the insurance protection of plaintiffs and defendants. Thus, a Dutch person who is protected under a liability policy and who caused an accident which injured an uninsured man will be forced to pay more than would have been awarded if the roles had been reversed. French courts sometimes express sympathy for financially distressed accident victims by quietly relating awards to defendants' ability to pay. Norwegian courts, too, alleviate victims' financial problems by ordering wealthy defendants to pay damages.

A small-scale movement in the Italian courts toward considering ability-to-pay indicates that corporations will pay larger amounts of damages than such defendants have paid in the past. Moreover, it probably will prove to be the predecessor of similar shifts in Latin American and elsewhere. In Italy, as in many countries, courts have been more concerned with indemnifying wealthy and prominent accident victims adequately than with forcing corporations to pay damages commensurate with their enviable financial conditions. In decisions of recent years, however, Italians lacking in money and influence have won awards from corporations so high as to suggest strongly that the courts had compared their capacities to absorb losses with the defendants' ability to pay damages.

Pain and suffering

A standard practice in the United States, which also is employed by the courts of most other countries, is awarding for pain and emotional disturbance. The courts of Norway and Spain are exceptions, but in estimating long-term losses Spanish jurists sometimes inject sympathy into their calculations of awards for long-term income replacement to plaintiffs who have suffered grievously.

While acceptance of the idea that awards for damages should include allowances for the victims' physical or mental distress is widespread, the amounts awarded currently are not sufficiently large to cause much concern to prospective corporate defendants in countries other than the United States and Canada: awards for pain and suffering exceeding the equivalent of $10,000 have been rare. In Europe, most liberal courts in this regard are those of Germany and the United Kingdom—the countries where allowance for pain and suffering began decades ago.

More important than present levels of awards for intangible costs and the prospect of higher levels, however, is the probability that relating awards to suffering will lead to greater numbers of damages suits in almost all countries. Awards which greatly exceed plaintiff's monetary losses are windfalls, and news of windfalls prompt many to sue.

The Contingent Fee

An indirect but powerful influence upon levels of liability awards in the United States has been the contingent fee system of charging for lawyers' services. Commonly, under this speculative basis of compensation, lawyers receive 35 percent of the awards or settlements. The inducement to strive for huge awards is evident.

Abroad, the contingent fee plan is usually regarded by the few persons who know of it as a bizarre American phenomenon. With exceptions such as those indicated above in the section, "Contingent Fee System," plaintiffs' lawyers are paid on the basis of negotiated flat fees or court-prescribed charges. And, as indicated also in that section, conversion to the contingent fee is not at all likely.

Future Climates of Legal Liability

The legal liability climate of any country in the future may differ from that of the present because of a single change in attitudes and acts of legislators, judges, lawyers, and ordinary citizens. A highly restrictive codified system of tort law may have been loosened by legislation or by systematic circumvention in the courts. Redistribution of property and income via awards for damages may have become a mission of the courts. The concept of negligence may have been reshaped by adoption of concepts and doctrines such as attractive nuisance and dangerous instrumentality. Applicability of the standard of strict liability may have been drastically broadened. Damages awards may have become fully reflective of accident victims' losses in both the short and long runs. Awards for physical and mental suffering may have exceeded those for out-of-pocket losses in numerous instances.

Workmen's Compensation Costs

In almost all countries, the most costly form of strict liability, by wide margins, holds employers liable for job-related disabilities.

Current Costs

While costs to employers of employees' occupational disabilities are at least as high in all other industrial countries as in the United States, they attract less managerial attention elsewhere. The main reason is that they are obscured by including workmen's compensation in government social security systems. In most countries, government agencies administer wage replacement and hospital-medical benefits without distinguishing between needs developing from employment and those occurring in other ways. An additional reason for managerial disinterest in workmen's compensation costs is the basing of employers' social security taxes solely on wages. Because it cannot reduce workmen's compensation costs by preventing accidents, management concerns itself with other costs.

Whether readily calculable or not, occupational disability costs represent significant percentages of payrolls in all countries. However, they differ greatly from country to country because of differences in benefits, with breadth of protection the most important. While the compensation systems of most countries provide both hospital-medical and wage replacement benefits, a few exceptions exist. Denmark pays wage replacement benefits only, with cooperative societies bearing hospital-medical costs.[13] Venezuela's plan covers only hospital and medical costs. However, in those areas of the country in which the government has no hospitals or clinics, no benefits whatever are paid and employees who suffer job-connected disabilities in those areas are compensated only if they are successful in suing their employers.[14]

Differences in the levels of benefits also are significant. While most systems provide whatever medical care is needed, some pay only in event of severe injuries. Venezuela's law, for example, bars benefits unless disability exceeds 5 percent. In the area of wage replacement, many systems provide for replacement of two-thirds of lost income. Commonly, however, the specified percentages have little meaning because of supplementary provisions of the laws. Thus, Swedish law specifies replacement of 66⅔ percent of lost earnings and requires that employers make supplementary direct payments during disabilities of ninety or fewer days, raising combined recoveries to essentially 100 percent. Under Italian law, conversely, the 100 percent wage replacement provision is qualified by a ceiling amounting to $750 per year. For a high-salaried Italian, therefore, the plan provides grossly inadequate benefits.

Contributing to differences in both hospital-medical and wage replacement benefits are differences in bearing losses resulting from accidents occurring off the employers' premises. In the United States and in most other countries, employees injured en route to their places of employment rarely qualify for workmen's compensation benefits. In Belgium, France, Germany, Mexico, Spain, and Sweden, however, such accidents are regarded as having occurred in the course of employment.

Benefit patterns differ also in accordance with employers' obligations to bear costs of benefits supplementing workmen's compensation or social security. As indicated above, the added benefits afforded victims of short-term disabilities in Sweden are paid by employers. In France, Germany, Norway, and Spain, among others, laws require that employees injured through gross negligence of their employers receive extra benefits therefrom.[15] Under the Italian version, the negligent employer must provide the benefits which the government would have borne if the accident had been caused in some other manner. Because recoveries from the two governmental providers of workmen's compensation in Italy often are long delayed, injured employees commonly attempt to recover under negligence claims from employers who actually had been blameless. Disabled Mexican employees can sue their employers for damages even though they have received social security benefits. Few have exercised that right, but if a general upswing in suits for damages develops in Mexico, it will consist in part of claims brought by employees against their employers.

Penalization of employers under laws like those outlined above is a departure from the most basic of workmen's compensation principles, i.e., entitlement of disabled employees to benefits without regard to negligence. No indications that governments regret that deviation and soon will eliminate the penalties are evident.

Not all the supplementary costs borne by employers are imposed by law. In some countries employers are driven by compassion, competition, or pressure from unions to provide health insurance to compensate for deficiencies in the government plans. Many employers in Italy, for example, buy commercial insurance in the expectation that their employees will experience delays of unpredictable length in recovering from the government's insurance companies. In Venezuela, white collar employees are not covered by the state plan. Faced by a shortage of managerial personnel, Venezuela employers attempt to retain or recruit such persons by offering private insurance protection against the costs of job-caused disability.

Future Costs

Because wage replacement benefits ordinarily relate to payrolls, costs of workmen's compensation benefits must rise as payrolls rise. However, while payrolls seem likely to rise in many countries through the late seventies and early eighties, increases in costs of workmen's compensation are not likely to be as great as increases in liability losses and liability insurance premiums. Moreover, in almost all countries, incidences of suit for damages will increase more than frequencies of on-the-job accidents. However, liability losses are not likely to draw close to workmen's compensation costs in any country during the next several decades. For industrial employers abroad, costs of job-caused disabilities will equal from 1 to 5 percent of payrolls. Their cost of coping with the liability peril probably will not exceed 0.5 percent of their payrolls.

NOTES

1. Indicative of the relative freedom from concern which manufacturers of nonconsumable products still enjoy in these countries was a recent development in Belgium. Many auto owners there believed that in following an oil company's advice

to add an oil to their gasoline they had damaged their engines. Nevertheless, not a single suit for damages was filed, for Belgians recognized that their courts would demand such clear proof that the additive alone was the cause of the damage as to make suing uneconomical.

2. Some of the prohibitory statutes antedate the development of the contingent fee system in the United States and were not enacted in disapproval of the principle of contingent pricing. Danish law provides that the courts fix lawyers' fees, and a Norwegian statute specifies a scale of fees relating to levels of the courts involved.

3. Germans, during the years immediately following World War II, were exposed in an unusual manner to the legal liability climate of the United States. When German and United States citizens were jointly involved in accidents, American-staffed courts had jurisdiction. The courts mirrored the attitudes and procedures in tort cases in the United States. A direct and all-important consequence of the lessons learned by Germans during that period has been that German courts now grant damages for pain and suffering.

4. The statement is included in the French Civil Code.

5. Roscoe Pound, *The Spirit of the Common Law* (Boston: Marshall Jones Company, 1921), p. 3.

6. Moreover, portions of a few countries differ in this regard from the countries' general positions. Courts of the Spanish province of Catalonia, for example, refer to no codes whatever, while courts in the remainder of the country are committed to use of the civil code.

7. While the municipality can, under an ordinance, impose fines upon property owners who fail to remove ice and snow from public sidewalks, the basic responsibility for care of the public way rests with the municipality. Consequently, an injured passerby usually is advised by his lawyers to sue the city rather than the owner of the adjacent property.

8. Only eleven states have prescribed the comparative negligence rule by statute, but many courts throughout the country have handed down decisions reflecting the comparative negligence principle.

9. Illustrative was a Spanish court's dismissal of a suit for damages in the amount of the equivalent of $1,000 by a woman who lost her hair for two years as a result, allegedly, of a permanent improperly administered by a hairdresser.

10. In none of them, however, have the courts been receptive to the concept of dangerous instrumentality.

11. Interest in the finding of Cutter Laboratories, Incorporated, liable for deaths of children in the United States following polio vaccine injections, despite the court's admission of inability to detect negligence in the production of the vaccine, has been world-wide.

12. The Mexican code does not set a limit upon awards relating to property damage. At least one such award has exceeded the equivalent of $40,000. Brazil's code, too, limits only bodily injury awards.

13. Each Dane must be a member of such a society. The societies pay benefits without differentiating between occupational and nonoccupational costs. Employers pay nothing to the societies directly but contribute heavily to their support via governmental subsidies.

14. Persons working in areas of Mexico in which governmental medical care is not available likewise must move directly against their employers. Under the labor codes applicable to such disability situations, incidentally, employees' recoveries

tend to be larger than those which otherwise would have been provided under social security.

15. Under Spain's elective system, the disabled employee has the option of accepting the benefits afforded under the social security system (plus the indicated supplementation on occasion) or suing for damages. The suit route has been little used.

4

TRENDS RELATING TO PERIL OF THEFT

In every country, commercial, financial, and industrial companies are exposed to three forms of theft—embezzlement, burglary and robbery, and sneak thievery. "Embezzlement" here refers to theft of property of any kind by employees from employers. "Burglary" applies to the taking of property following forcible entry, and "robbery," to theft involving use of physical force or threat thereof against persons. Extortion is robbery from a victim on a continuing basis and therefore is included here in the term "robbery." "Sneak thievery" includes such crimes as shoplifting, stealing unattended property, hijacking, and swindling.

This chapter is concerned with the costs of theft, now and in the future, to companies operating outside the United States. "Costs" consist of losses and of expenditures for prevention and insurance. Another function of the chapter is to identify the determinants of the levels of such costs.

Present Cost of Theft

The cost of theft in commerce and industry varies greatly from country to country. In some countries, great segments of the populace seemingly await opportunities to steal. In others, apparently, very few persons are even tempted to steal. Variances in the significance of theft also occur within each country. The sections below categorize various countries in terms of predominant conditions.

Embezzlement

In any country, measuring the aggregate losses to embezzlers for a given period of time is impossible. Unknown numbers of embezzlers succeed in keeping their employers unaware that their property has been stolen. Commonly, management is unable to estimate the portions of shortages attributable to embezzlement, shoplifting, and faulty record-keeping. In many countries, therefore, embezzlements may occur much more frequently than is generally believed. Consequently, the insignificant levels of embezzlement indicated below for some countries should be regarded with some skepticism.

Pilferage

"Pilferage" here refers to employees' stealing their employers' tools and items from other inventories. While the term could apply to theft by employees acting in collaboration with each other, it will relate here only to simple and solitary acts such as an employee's walking off the premises with a pair of pliers concealed in his pocket. (Collaborative thefts will be treated in a section below.)

The only observation presented here with full assurance is that employee pilferage occurs in all countries. However earnestly morality is stressed and however severe the punishment, no society is immune to this (or any other) form of theft.

Eventually, perhaps, communication will progress so far that the people of all countries will resemble each other in attitudes and behavior so closely that the incidence of employee pilferage everywhere will be about the same. At present, however, pilferage appears to be a much more costly part of doing business in some countries than in others. Losses seem particularly high in Argentina, Brazil, Chile, France, Mexico, Sweden, and Venezuela. In these countries, losses are so high that well-managed companies in almost all industries routinely include compensatory charges in their prices.

On a lower level of cost are countries in which pilferage occurs in many industries but rarely constitutes a significant drain. Countries in this category are Belgium, Denmark, Germany, Norway, and the United Kingdom. Pilferers are few and have such low levels of thievish ambition that they take only the most stealable items. The elements of stealability are: (a) size so small as to afford concealment in a cupped hand, pocket, or purse, (b) unit values so low that the employer cannot afford to be greatly concerned over loss of a few units daily, and (c) direct usefulness to the pilferer. Particularly stealable are such items as aspirin tablets, birth control pills, ballpoint pens, pliers, candy bars, and spark plugs.

Aggregate losses from pilfering are lowest in those countries in which such thefts occur mostly in a few industries or in a few geographical areas. The principal victims are in construction and in transportation.[1] Many managers in every country believe that their companies are virtually immune to employee pilferage, but specialists directly concerned with theft regard that view as naive. Indeed, the specialists feel that employee pilferage is on the lowest level of significance in very few countries. Of the countries considered in this study, only in the Netherlands and in Spain is pilferage negligible.

Effort to prevent pilferage and to detect it early is limited mainly to surveillance by foremen, posting guards at plant gates, and use of check-out systems in issuing tools and maintenance equipment. Expenditures for such measures differ from country to country, but the differences in cost do not seem to be as wide as the differences in losses.

Almost no employers buy insurance applicable to employee pilferage. While some might desire it, insurers almost universally regard the peril as uninsurable.

Lone wolf manipulative embezzlement

Whereas pilferage is a simple form of theft, manipulative embezzlement entails use of more or less complex techniques for stealing by falsifying records relating to payrolls, receivables, disbursements, billings, investments, dividend distributions, and other accounts. In most cases, manipulative embezzlers are executives, administrative technicians, or clerical employees, but the term "white-collar thief" is not always descriptive; machine operators, construction foremen, warehouse laborers, truck drivers, and persons in many other blue-collar jobs have stolen by manipulating their employers' records.

As the subheading indicates, this section relates only to stealing by a manipulator who acts without assistance from other employees. In this form of embezzlement, countries can be placed in two categories. In one, discovered losses are sufficiently large and numerous to keep management aware of the peril. In the other, losses are so seldom uncovered that management recognizes no such peril.[2] Most countries are in the first category, with loss levels differing only slightly. Of the countries considered in this study, only Italy, Japan, and Spain seem to belong in the second category, and Italy may be a marginal qualifier.

Contrary to the widespread assumption that incidences of theft of all forms are much higher in Latin American countries than in other areas in which United States-based companies are active, one-man manipulative embezzlements probably occur no more frequently in Latin America than in France, the United Kingdom, and Sweden and only slightly more frequently than in the other countries of nothern Europe.

Programs of prevention and early detection of embezzlements by lone wolf manipulators (and by rings of employee thieves, as well) consist, in virtually all countries other than the United States, of routine audits by internal and external accountants. As in the United States, however, auditors elsewhere do not regard embezzlement control as one of their main responsibilities. Therefore, the amounts of money spent by affiliates and owner companies alike on auditing for that purpose are very small.

Insurance is available in almost all countries for protecting employers against losses from manipulative embezzlers. Premium rates abroad are high in comparison with those charged in the United States because insurers assume that the employers which buy the protection are particularly exposed to loss and that their losses must be spread over small numbers of policyholders.

Collusive embezzlement

Less common everywhere than one-man embezzlements are complex thefts involving two or more employees and, frequently, outsiders. Participating in a collusive embezzlement may be persons engaged in diverse forms of work. A director of purchasing, a computer programmer, a laborer in the receiving department, and a truck driver may have roles in a system for stealing from their employer's incoming shipments. Although employers in several countries have lost heavily in such thefts, aggregate losses through collusion probably are considerably lower everywhere than those resulting from either employee pilferage or lone wolf manipulations. With numerous persons involved, secrecy is difficult to maintain. Hence, collusive embezzlements ordinarily function only briefly before being uncovered or voluntarily terminated by apprehensive participants.

Embezzlements of this category seemingly occur mainly in the countries of northern Europe, with companies in France and the United Kingdom having suffered the largest individual losses.

Other Forms of Theft

Robbery occurs in all countries but is a peril of significance to corporations in very few. In France, the United Kingdom, and Venezuela, banks, operators of supermarkets, and companies paying their employees in cash are exposed to comparatively high probabilities of loss.[3] Other countries in western Europe—Belgium, Italy, and Sweden, in particular—have had startling but short-lived outbreaks of robbery.[4] Elsewhere, almost all robbery loss has been suffered by individuals and proprietors of small stores.

Burglary losses and costs of guarding against burglary are substantial for companies in all countries. Even in those few countries in which burglaries of large companies are uncommon, most companies must employ watchmen, bar windows and doors, and maintain alarm systems. Also indicative of the breadth of concern is the insuring against burglary by large numbers of domestically controlled companies which do not use fidelity bonds as protection against embezzlement. Those practices prevail in Belgium, Denmark, Italy, Norway, and Spain. Burglary losses are particularly large in France, Sweden, the United Kingdom, and the Latin American countries.

Sneak thievery accounts for losses exceeding those from any other form of theft in every country considered in this study. The losses, however, constitute virtually the full cost of sneak thievery, for companies in most countries spend very little to prevent sneak thievery and less on insurance.[5] In terms of losses and preventive expenditures, sneak thievery probably costs less in most countries than embezzlement and burglary. Exceptions seem to be Denmark, the Netherlands, and Spain, where incidence of sneak thievery—although not high in comparison with other European countries—greatly outweigh those of either burglary or embezzlement.

Pilferage by dock workers and trespassers occurs in all ports. Because shippers and their insurers seldom are indemnified for such losses by ship owners or terminal operators, pilferage is a substantial drain upon almost all companies using port facilities. Pilferers favor goods having high ratios of value to bulk, but they are not averse to stealing such heavy items as major components of earth-moving vehicles, machine tools, and other massive pieces of equipment. Losses are much greater in ports in which organized gangs operate than in ports in which thieves ordinarily steal individually and opportunistically. While organized pilfering occurs in the ports of many countries, it is especially costly in Chile, France, Mexico, and the United Kingdom. Countries in which port pilferage is committed mainly by solitary thieves are Denmark, Germany, the Netherlands, Norway, and Spain.

Not all pilferage of goods in transit occurs on docks. Goods are stolen from trucks and railroad cars, from rail, air, and truck depots, and from customs warehouses. Variances from country to country in these forms of pilferage are greater than those in seaports. In some— Chile, Mexico, and Venezuela, in particular—theft of goods in customs and in rail and truck terminals costs more in the aggregate than pilferage on the docks. Rarely in those countries do shippers recover from those who had lawful custody of the goods. Countries in which inland pilferage of goods in transit occurs frequently but is a less costly program than theft on the docks are Brazil, France, and the

United Kingdom. In the other countries considered here, losses by inland pilferage are considerably smaller than those occurring on the docks.

Motor vehicle theft plagues companies in all countries. Even in Denmark, the Netherlands, and Spain, where other kinds of theft are infrequent, car thefts are numerous. While frequency rates do not differ markedly from country to country, amounts of loss differ greatly because of dissimilar purposes behind the thefts. In some countries, almost all auto thefts are committed by youths who abandon the vehicles within hours. While such amateur thieves often damage the cars, the losses usually are less than total. Almost all the vehicle thefts in the three countries listed above and in Italy, Norway, and Sweden as well, are of that variety, and aggregate losses to corporate owners (and their insurers), therefore, are not great. In Belgium, France, Germany, and the United Kingdom, however, high proportions of vehicle thefts are committed by professionals for purpose of sale. Recoveries of vehicles taken by those thieves are rare, and losses therefore are considerably higher in those countries than elsewhere.

A form of unorganized motor vehicle theft costing much more than temporary loss of use is looting. In Brazil, Mexico, and Venezuela, many cars and trucks which have been left unattended briefly have been stripped of most of their removable components by local opportunists. Few corporate owners of vehicles lose heavily in that manner, but using insurance to cover the possibility of stripping and spending liberally on vehicle maintenance in order to minimize the likelihood of roadside breakdowns are costs relating to the peril.

Shoplifting is the most costly part of the theft peril to operators of large stores everywhere. In almost all countries, shoplifting losses became substantial when stores grew large enough to be divided into departments. Scandinavian merchants for many years suffered lesser losses than their counterparts elsewhere, but their experience since the early sixties has been about that of store owners elsewhere in Europe. While losses differ somewhat from country to country, the proclivity to steal from merchants seems to occur almost uniformly. The principal factor in differences in loss probably is deterrence by managerial surveillance.

Shoplifters differ from country to country. In some countries, thrill-seeking youths are the principal offenders. In others, the typical shoplifter is a person of middle age who steals to finance an addiction. In still others the poor shoplift in desperation. Whatever the circumstances of the shoplifters, owners of large stores in every country face the same grim fact: if they do not spend heavily to prevent shoplifting, they may eventually become insolvent.

In addition to the standard forms of sneak thievery outlined above, local varieties—some of them bizarre—impose their costs in numerous countries. Thus, a company had barely completed laying a surface pipeline for transporting water to its plant in a rural area of Venezuela before residents of the area shot holes in the pipe in order to fill their water needs. After learning that plugging the holes and admonishing the water thieves accomplished nothing, the company fitted taps to some of the holes and permitted the residents to draw water at will.

Circumstances behind Theft

Behind a theft may be anything from a single, readily identified condition to a combination of obscure conditions. Examined below are the circumstances prevalent in various countries and their consequences.

Environmental Conditions and Developments

Expansion of social security systems

Commonly, in countries which are experiencing more thievery now than in the past and which have established comprehensive systems of social security businessmen attribute the first of those developments to the second. In particular, they blame social security for theft by youths, holding that many persons who have spent their first two decades under governmental guarantees against economic want have come to believe that they are entitled to protection against economic problems of all kinds. Consequently, these observers reason, the eighteen-year-old who is embittered by society's failure to provide him with an expensive car readily rationalizes stealing to finance the purchase of one.

However, proof that social security systems are a major cause of theft is elusive. Clearly, theft is a more costly problem in the United Kingdom, with a history of three decades of comprehensive sheltering under social security, than in Spain, where the social security system is newer and much less comprehensive. Conversely, some forms of theft are considerably more troublesome in Mexico than in Belgium, even though the latter's social security system is broader and older. Also, while theft is a greater problem in Sweden than in Norway, the social security programs of the two do not differ greatly in comprehensiveness or age. Eventually, conclusive evidence on the subject may be assembled. Until then, the collective opinion of risk controllers and insurance brokers may be as credible as any: it holds that highly developed social security systems are a factor in the proclivity of some to steal but that combinations of other conditions are much more powerful influences.

Other laws

While social security systems may or may not affect the incidence of theft, other laws clearly have done so. A Danish statute describes auto thieves as unauthorized borrowers, and Spanish law states that they have obtained involuntary loans. Under both laws, thieves must pay repair costs if they have damaged stolen vehicles. Otherwise, they are essentially immune to punishment if the owners soon regain use of their cars.

Brazilian law bestows a form of tenure upon an employee who has worked for ten years for the same employer. Dismissal of a tenured employee, even upon evidence of embezzlement, is very difficult. Consequently, some employees who refrained from stealing from their employers during the first ten years in their jobs begin embezzling thereafter. Others begin stealing after nine years in anticipation of being fired, in accordance with common practice, shortly before completion of their tenth year. Under Italy's severance rights law, an employee discharged after only a few years of working for a single employer receives a modest stipend. If, however, he is fired after seven years—even for theft—his allowance amounts to almost the total of his earnings for the preceding two years. Consequently, the law both discourages and promotes embezzlement. During his first seven years of work for an employer, the employee tends to resist temptation to steal; the prospect of forfeiting the substantial severance allowance by misbehavior discourages theft. However, upon qualifying for the seventh-year allowance some employees become much less concerned about the prospect of dismissal and begin to steal.

A right-of-search law in the United Kingdom deters employee pilferage by granting employers the right to examine the contents of employees' pockets as they leave their working places. Similarly, a Mexican law is a deterrent because it permits the frisking of employees as they pass through plant gates.

Communist activity

Companies based in the United States face the possibility of loss of their entire investments in some countries through expropriation following Communist takeovers, but consideration below is limited to lesser seizures of corporate property.

The extent of theft loss attributable to subversive activity in a given country cannot be measured. Police have identified bank holdups and payroll robberies as fund raising efforts of Communists. Mainly, they have occurred in Latin American companies, Belgium, and Italy. To assume that none of those thefts would have occurred if Communist doctrine had not driven believers to make such attacks on private capital, however, probably would be unrealistic. Some of the thieves might have committed robbery and burglary even if they had not joined Communist groups. The chief impact of Communism upon theft, therefore, might have been that of a catalyst which motivated small numbers of persons to join with numerous career thieves in this form of financing their cause.

Poverty

The forms of theft commonly attributed to poverty are burglary and sneak thievery. Neither, in any country, is committed exclusively by the poor. When jobs outnumbered workers in Belgium, France, and Sweden during the sixties, for example, sneak thievery and burglary (as well as robbery and embezzlement) by regularly employed persons were rather common. In many countries, however, those who spend their lives on the edge of starvation tend to regard sneak thievery or burglary as part-time occupations to which they were consigned by fate.[6] Consequently, where lifelong isolation from the labor force is commonplace, the incidences of those forms of crime are high.

Conversely, high levels of chronic unemployment are deterrents to embezzlement. The reason, presumably, is that employed persons in countries thus afflicted do not risk losing their jobs by embezzling. This deterrence has been evident in Italy.

Temptation

One of the most important determinants of the number of thefts in any country is the number of opportunities to steal with little likelihood of capture. Such temptation bears particularly upon the incidence of employee pilferage. Where such crime is rare, managers tend to give credit to the formidable difficulties confronting would-be pilferers rather than to honesty. Managers in Belgium, Denmark, and Norway point out the deterrence inherent in the small sizes of their countries. A person fired for embezzling in a small country, they note, will experience great difficulty in finding a new job. Also, a pilferer who fled to avoid arrest can hide only briefly in a small population.

Relevant, too, is the size of the employee group in which a prospective pilferer works. In all countries, companies operating small units tend to lose less to pilferers than those employing many persons. Whereas employees of large companies are indifferent to the behavior of fellow workers, workers in small companies tend to be interested in misdeeds on the job. In small companies, therefore, management learns early of even petty pilferage.

The nature of an employer's product also is a factor in the incidence of embezzlement. Even where nationwide losses through employee pilferage are very low, companies suffer large losses if they manufacture or distribute especially stealable products. A stealable product is small, light, and widely useful.

Burglars and sneak thieves find commonplace goods attractive because they can steal them easily and sell them easily. In the United Kingdom, for example, companies shipping tires, cigarettes, motorcycles, TV sets, whiskey, and a variety of other widely used products lose heavily to thieves on the docks, in warehouses, and on the highways. The thieves can readily sell such items at prices close to those in the legitimate retail markets. Operating throughout Latin America are no-questions-asked markets affording salability of goods of almost every kind. A victim who desires to regain his property quite possibly will be able to repurchase it in the local thieves' market a day or two after the theft. Obviously, the presence of such a market tempts many to commit burglary or sneak thievery.

Indicative of the relative disinterest of thieves in property which is not generally useful is the rarity of thefts of machine tools and computers—however valuable and however portable.

In no country do many robberies seem to be attributable to temptation. The few exceptions are holdups committed by criminals who believe that they have found extraordinarily vulnerable possessors of cash. Undermanned transporters of payroll cash continue to invite robbery. Solitary merchants and unguarded banks are likewise tempting targets. And as operation of grocery supermarkets spreads, casual handling of cash by such stores will, increasingly, be irresistible to robbers.

Immigration

Australian companies have reported that they lost more property to thieves during the years 1967–76 than in any other decade. Embezzlement, burglary, robbery (sometimes joined with murder), and extortion occurred in dismaying numbers. Particularly disturbing have been indications of organized crime. According to employees of insurance companies which have paid large sums of money to corporate victims of such crimes, a reason for the increases has been post-World War II immigration of thousands of Europeans. The insurers' finding probably is well founded, inasmuch as they cannot long remain solvent if they do not know the causes of their losses.

However, situations in Belgium, Germany, and the Netherlands during the sixties produced quite different conclusions. Employers in those countries coped with shortages of workers by hiring many thousands of citizens of the countries from which Australia's immigrants came. While the employers may have lost some property to their temporary employees, they were certain that such losses were insignificant.

Mental Processes

In addition to the environmental circumstances noted above, the mental processes of thieves, ordinary citizens, and judges determine the frequency and severity of theft losses.

Thieves

While a complete account of the mental processes behind a person's stealing may never be written, the inner forces which most commonly cause theft are perceptible. In the countries considered in this study, the most potent forces seem to be the following: innate criminality, costly compulsions, youthful thirst for excitement, youthful contempt for ordinary standards of behavior, indifference to rights of others, and elevated expectations.

In every population are persons who seem committed to a lifetime of theft. Some are career thieves, whether stealing crudely or with great finesse. Many more are amateurs who do not try to support themselves solely by theft, even though they may employ planning and techniques like those of professionals. Other persons steal in desperate efforts to satisfy cravings for gambling, alcohol, or narcotics. While alcoholism leads to stealing in all countries, it seems to occur most commonly in northern Europe and in countries inhabited mainly by persons of northern European ancestry. Most shoplifting in France, Sweden, and the United Kingdom probably is committed by alcoholics. Conversely, little sneak thievery or any other form of stealing occurs in Italy, Spain, and Latin American countries for the purpose of satisfying cravings for alcohol. On the proportionate basis, more embezzlement and sneak thievery is blamed upon compulsive gamblers in the United Kingdom than in the other countries considered here. Stealing by narcotics addicts is a much more costly problem for companies in the United States than for affiliates in any of the countries indicated in this study, in none of which had it become a significant cost by the mid-seventies.

The principal force behind stealing by the young of many countries is need for illicit excitement. Where widespread theft by youths has developed only since the mid-fifties, the thieves basically have been seeking thrills. The trend seemed to develop mainly in countries in which long periods of prosperity had shielded almost all young persons from severe economic deprivation. The most troubled countries in this regard have been Belgium, Denmark, France, Italy, the Netherlands, Norway, and the United Kingdom. In other prosperous countries, conditions have developed which offset the trend. In Sweden, bored youths probably would have committed many more thefts if they had not feared tough police forces. In Germany, Japan, and Spain, where stealing by youths has not approached the levels indicated above, parental or religious influences seem to have dampened hunger for excitement via theft.

A worrisome development which began in the mid-fifties in many countries has been the growing contempt with which many youth view long-established codes of conduct. It is manifested by irresponsibility and law breaking and, in particular, has underlain much of the stealing from companies by young persons. It seems to have been especially virulent in countries in which theft has been a response also to widespread desire for excitement. And in countries like Germany, Japan, and Spain, the countervailing forces which prevented youth from stealing to satisfy need of excitement have also prevented them from scorning traditional patterns of behavior.

Although indifference to rights of others is a part of the mentality of almost every thief, many thieves hold ambivalent attitudes toward property rights of others. Thus, a person may steal without compunction from his employer—viewing small-scale embezzlement as a perquisite of employment—but feel no inclination whatever to steal from any other company or person. (The bulk of employee pilfering in most countries, probably, is committed by persons thus motivated.) Another may steal with great satisfaction from companies while scrupulously honoring the property rights of individuals. Or an employee may delight in pilfering occasionally from his employer's inventories but reject an opportunity to participate in a large-scale embezzlement.

Some thieves, conversely, are mentally equipped to steal as much as possible from any person or company. Their atittude is summarized in the creed of Mexican sneak thieves: "If any owner does not guard his property, he desires it less than I, and my theft of it is therefore proper." This attitude toward property rights seems to occur more commonly in Brazil, Chile, Italy, Mexico, and Venezuela than in the other countries considered here.

Upon achieving even brief periods of comparative prosperity, some persons unconsciously raise their economic aspirations markedly. Persons in Mexico, Chile, and other Latin American countries who become wage earners after years spent virtually without receiving or spending cash develop new desires for possessions, including the ultimate in desirable things—autos. Commonly their earnings do not keep pace with their soaring aspirations, and the result for some is frustration so bitter that they turn to theft for supplemental income.

The extent to which companies' losses to thieves in any country result from unrealistic expectations probably cannot be measured. However, in all countries in which large numbers of persons recently have made economic gains which were unprecedented in their experience, a significant pressure to steal must be assumed. Countering it in part will be fear of losing jobs, but many persons will have become permanently dependent upon theft.

Ordinary citizens

Although the attitudes of thieves have a greater effect upon levels of theft, the attitudes of ordinary, honest persons toward stealing are influential. In countries in which law-abiding citizens typically regard thieves with tolerance (except, of course, when they have been the victims), their pressure upon police, courts, and legislatures to control theft closely is negligible. Moreover, such tolerance encourages theft by those only marginally disposed to steal.

Tolerant citizens are especially numerous in France, Italy, and the Latin American countries.[7] In particular, persons in those countries shrug off such crimes as employees' stealing things of small value and youths' stealing cars or shoplifting.

Judges

Attitudes of the judges who hear theft charges also affect patterns of theft. Because judges find guilt and impose the sentence for theft under statutory constraints, some of their influence is derived from the attitudes of legislators. However, they do exercise judgment, and some thereby discourage stealing while others encourage it.

In a few countries the judiciary is consistently severe in its findings and its sentencing. Because of their readiness to impose the maximum sentence, judges in Germany, the Netherlands, and the United Kingdom probably do more than their counterparts in the other countries considered here to dissuade people from stealing. And they do not penalize first offenders so lightly that the citizenry assumes that the law forgives each person his first theft. Conversely, judges in Norway and Spain rule less harshly against first offenders although they deal severely with thieves of all other categories.

Also contrasting with the harsh attitudes is the tolerance of judges in Brazil, Denmark, Italy, Mexico, Sweden, and Venezuela. In accordance with the codes, or with their own views, they commonly place even thieves with records of prior convictions on probation unless the criminals injured their victims. Moreover, they rarely hand down prison sentences exceeding two years to those having records of many convictions and regularly terminate the longer sentences by placing the thieves on parole after a few months. Contributing to the tolerance in those countries is the view that poverty as a condition of life warrants short sentences. Indeed, if the thieves who stole from their employers are poor, the judges are so sympathetic that they are most unlikely to hand down prison sentences.

Management

Attitudes of managers bear significantly upon corporate losses to thieves. Within every country managers differ in their opinions as to amounts of losses which might occur and the means of dealing with thieves. Nevertheless, each country has predominant attitudes. Outlined below are characteristic attitudes of native-born managers in countries other than the United States.

In the United States, many in management make the mistake of assuming that persons with whom they long have worked cannot be embezzling. Rarely, however, are American managers so naïve as to assume that none of their company's employees are disposed to steal. On the contrary, throughout Europe the typical executive realizes that some companies incur embezzlement but regards it as a peril of no significance in his own company. His employer has never uncovered a major embezzlement and believes its losses through employee pilferage to be trifling.

German and British managers seem to be more aware of the possibilities of severe loss from embezzlement than managers elsewhere in Europe, but ordinarily even they are only mildly concerned. Britons have been startled by major embezzlements in the sixties and seventies but remain confident that their companies' internal and external audit systems will prevent significant losses. Most disregard the fact that determined thieves have the time, and sometimes the resourcefulness, to circumvent the most advanced accounting controls. German managers tend to regard as potential embezzlers only those who handle large flows of cash or otherwise have obvious opportunities to steal, despite evidence that employees holding all kinds of jobs have participated in large embezzlements in the United States and elsewhere.

Managers throughout Latin America worry more about employee theft than Europeans. Mainly they are concerned with employee pilferage, perhaps assuming that their countrymen lack the patience and secretiveness necessary for perpetrating large-scale, collusive embezzlements. Therefore, they attempt to cope with employee dishonesty principally by requiring employees to submit to routine frisking as they file out of their working places. By doing without practices designed to make prolonged concealment of complex embezzlements very difficult, they encourage such stealing.

Prosecution does not necessarily follow identification of embezzlers in the United States, and managers in other countries are even less inclined to seek arrests. This attitude prevails even in Italy and the United Kingdom, where employers who do not prosecute forfeit their rights to recover under their fidelity bonds. It stems in Europe from fear of the adverse publicity which would be generated by prosecution, and in Brazil, Mexico, and Venezuela from certainty that the courts would not administer punishment even upon admission of guilt.[8]

Norwegian employers commonly do not even fire embezzlers, preferring to seek reimbursement from future earnings of the thieves. Reportedly, many have recovered in full.

Few managers believe that embezzlement could destroy their companies. In all countries, however, most managers recognize that losses through burglary, robbery, and sneak thievery can be severe.[9] Consequently, manufacturers direct their expenditures for crime prevention mainly toward these lesser perils, employing watchmen and installing alarm systems, fencing, illumination, and barred windows. Likewise, retailers train employees to detect and discourage shoplifters. Except in the United States and Canada, few managers realize that internal thieves might be much more destructive to profits than thieves in all other categories.

Future Costs of Theft in Foreign Affiliates

Affiliates of American corporations probably will not lose much more or much less to thieves in the eighties than in the seventies. In every country the attitudes and economic and social conditions which determine levels of theft are too persistent to permit sudden changes. However, the theft peril will change somewhat in every country.

Changes in Determinants

Increased use of computers will both reduce and increase theft losses. With all affiliates using computers in accounting, personnel administration, forecasting, production scheduling, production control, and other functions, opportunities for most employees to steal by manipulating records will be much less inviting than in the past. Overall, however, embezzlement losses may increase considerably, as computer programmers, operators, maintenance specialists, and supervisors take advantage of unprecedented opportunities to steal systematically from their employers. All companies using computers employ computer theft controls and, presumably, will be alert to improved protective techniques. However, the central facts in the history of embezzlement are that (a) dishonest employers are willing to spend more time in devising means of stealing than their employers will spend in anticipating new methods of theft; and (b) changes in personnel and operations endlessly present new opportunities to persons determined to embezzle. A forecaster was not at all reckless in predicting that the record corporate embezzlement in each country will prove to be one of computer fraud.

Another development which will increase thefts in the countries where it occurs is increase in population. If ratios of thieves to total population remain constant, the number of thieves in those countries whose population grows must rise. Probably, however, the increase in number of thieves will be out of proportion to the increase in general populations largely because of the explosive combination of rising economic aspirations of the poor and increasingly crowded housing. Among products of that combination will be fierce determination to acquire property and erosion of respect for property rights of others. Since population throughout Europe and in Japan has stabilized, those areas will not experience such stimuli to theft. Throughout Latin America and most of the other countries in which American companies operate affiliates, however, soaring populations will include ever larger number of thieves as well as spawn other important problems.

A trend which will bring reductions in theft losses is reduction in use of currency. As employers convert to paying wages by check and merchants accept customers' checks or credit cards, opportunities for remunerative burglary and robbery diminish.

The condition which will have the least predictable impact upon companies' losses to thieves is the repudiation by youth of the behavioral standards of their elders and their ancestors. If great numbers of young persons become contemptuous of those standards, many will steal. And if corrosive attitudes spread in the manner of physical corrosion, ever larger numbers of thieves will prey upon companies and individuals.

NOTES

1. In the transportation industry, most of the goods stolen belong not to the transportation companies employing the thieves but to shippers. Technically, such theft is not embezzlement. To the extent that a transportation company becomes liable to its customers for losses, however, the economic effect is that of embezzlement.
2. In numerous countries of both categories, the only companies insuring against the peril are those protected under policies secured by American owner corporations. In other countries, some domestically controlled companies insure but maintain limits much lower than those used in the United States.
3. Venezuela's robbery peril has exceeded that of the other Latin American countries only since the late fifties. It has been regarded mainly as a vehicle for fund raising by Communists.
4. Belgians and Swedes have blamed hold-up sprees upon foreigners (Americans and French) who were either apprehended or frightened into leaving for safer fields. In Italy, a series of hold-ups of Milan banks, occurring for a short time at the rate of one per day, shocked the entire country. Stationing armed guards in all banks in the city ended the episode, but insurers anticipate recurrences.
5. Insurance is available to cover only one form of sneak thievery, i.e., car theft.
6. Japan and Spain seem to be exceptions. In the latter, according to Spanish insurance executives, even the poorest persons are too proud to steal.
7. Brazilians may be more tolerant of human misdeeds than any other people. But other forces work there to discourage theft so that companies lose less to thieves of all kinds in Brazil than in numerous other countries.
8. Some United States-based companies regularly prosecute embezzlers in these and all other countries. The policy, however, reflects the attitudes of management in the United States, not that of nationals.
9. Exceptions are common. Thus, some French companies send elderly messengers on foot to deliver securities, jewelry, and other valuables. Similarly, many Brazilian and Mexican companies employ as bill collectors young men who travel carrying large amounts of cash, alone and unarmed, in rural areas.

5

TRENDS IN PHYSICAL HAZARDS

This chapter deals with natural and man-made hazards which threaten damage to corporate property outside the United States. Examined particularly are the hazards underlying the peril of fire. The underlying causes of damage by fire or explosion usually are indifference, carelessness, ignorance, and lack of foresight. Those deficiencies lead to incorporating hazards in new buildings and other facilities and to creating hazards in established facilities. Natural occurrences cause damage by exploiting inadequate protective measures and overwhelming the sturdiest of defenses.

In no country, of course, are physical hazards uniformly dangerous: winds fan fires more vigorously in one area than another; water pressures are sufficient for flatting the fiercest of fires in one city and woefully inadequate in another. Nevertheless, categorizing countries by predominant conditions is realistic.

Natural Hazards

Climate

A company planning to establish operations in numerous countries will encounter a wide range of climatic conditions. If, however, it already operates widely in the United States, it experiences approximately the same variances in precipitation, temperature, and wind as it will face overseas. Having ascertained the climatic patterns in a locality abroad where it is to establish an affiliate, therefore, it can draw upon its experience in an area of comparable climate in the United States in deciding how to cope with nature in the other country. Conversely, a company which has not had wide experience in the United States must seek guidance from persons familiar with climatic conditions in the country of the new affiliate.

Excesses or deficiencies in rainfall or other atmospheric moisture do not bear significantly upon probabilities of fire damage to industrial or commercial facilities inasmuch as they rarely are located near brush lands or forests which could become hazardous in periods of drought. High levels of precipitation or humidity, however, cause rusting, mildewing, warping, and discoloring. Goods in transit are particularly vulnerable, for packaging which can withstand the moisture in the place of manufacture may not protect adequately if the shipment is detained in a damper region. For example, goods shipped to Mexican cities in which humidity usually is low may be exposed to much dampness in the country's seaports and during transport through the lowlands. A shipment which had not been packaged to withstand extremely moist air could be ruined during a brief delay en route.

Wind velocities sufficient to damage machinery, buildings, vehicles, and goods in transit occur in all countries. In few countries, however, do the most destructive windstorms—typhoons, hurricanes, and tornadoes—occur so often and so fiercely as to require building extra measures of resistance into commercial and industrial structures. Major exceptions are the hurricanes which attack coastal cities in Mexico and Venezuela. Tornadoes occur so infrequently outside the tornado belts of the United States as to warrant no concern elsewhere.

The principal effect of temperatures upon the level of property damage is indirect. During especially cold and long winters in northern areas, wood interiors of some buildings are so dehydrated by artificial heat that fires spead very rapidly in them. The hazard is especially common in the Scandinavian countries, where wood is much used for paneling, framing, and flooring and where artificial heat may be needed for seven consecutive months. Even buildings equipped with heating systems which do not cause dehumidification may be subject to fire because of their proximity to dried-out structures.

Altitude, an atmospheric condition which is not technically one of weather but is associated with it, bears upon the amount of fire loss. The intensity with which fire burns depends partly upon the oxygen supply, and fire therefore spreads more slowly at high altitudes than at sea level. While management of a company planning to build a plant at an altitude of 6,000 feet cannot disregard the peril of fire in designing the buildings and plotting operations, it can assume that its fire control measures will be considerably more effective than if they were to be employed at an altitude of a few hundred feet.

Earthquake

In any country an earthquake can destroy buildings and equipment. However, the probabilities of destruction are very low except on those places on the earth's crust where mountain ranges are being raised or where other manifestations of the jostling of the colossal global plates are occurring. Under the stupendous compressive forces exerted, rock formations are subjected to stresses which ultimately exceed their capacity to resist or accommodate without bending or twisting. The formations thereupon fracture, and pent-up energy surges forth, vibrating the areas of the fractures and, perhaps, areas hundreds of miles distant.[1]

Fractures tend to occur in the vicinity of faults, i.e., earlier fractures in which the opposing sides were misaligned. Movements in portions of the crust where misalignments already exist virtually assure additional breakage. Natural history indicates that in areas in which fractures have occurred recently (within the past 10,000 years), additional breakage must be expected.[2] Many fractures in the several areas in which mountain ranges are being raised have occurred within the memory of man. Consequently, the areas in which major earthquakes can be expected have long been identified. The most active and most extensive of the seismic zones is the Circum-Pacific belt, stretching from the southernmost tip of Latin America, up the western mountain ranges of South, Central, and North America, across the Bering Strait, and down the Asian coasts and the island countries of the western Pacific through New Zealand. Almost 85 percent of all recorded earthquakes have been traced to fractures in that zone. Second in activity is the Alpide belt, which extends westward from Indonesia through the Himalayas and Mediterranean area into the Atlantic to an area west of the Azores. It has produced almost 15 percent of recorded earthquakes. Much less active zones are the Mid-Atlantic (a north-south belt) and the Mid-Indian (extending from ridges deep in the Indian Ocean into eastern areas of Africa).

Of the countries considered in this study, therefore, those particularly subject to the peril of earthquake are Italy, Japan, the Republic of the Philippines, Spain, southern France, and Venezuela.

Any building can be destroyed by earthquake, although steel frame structures and those of reinforced concrete which have been designed to withstand severe stresses will survive virtually all shocks. Steel frame construction is unusual in almost all countries, and, except in Japan, few large reinforced concrete buildings have been engineered to survive major earthquakes. In earthquake-prone countries, therefore, most industrial and commercial buildings are dangerously exposed to calamitous damage.

Fire Hazards Inherent in Construction
and Operations

Forms of Construction

In whatever country, the construction of a building largely determines the probability of extensive damage by fire to its structure, equipment, and inventories. The owner of a building in which fire is likely to occur bears a financial burden more or less commensurate with the probabilities of occurrence. The burden may take the form of insurance premiums, losses from fires, or spending for prevention.

However, even if a plant was designed and equipped to prevent large fires the owner bears a continuing cost. Its insurance premiums may reflect, to a degree, the vulnerability of the great majority of buildings. In theory, the owner should contribute through premium payments only toward losses in buildings similar to its own, but insurers sometimes err in classifying risks, with consequential forcing of some property owners to subsidize others. Moreover, presence of effective firefighting equipment may be outweighed as a factor of the premium rate by the fact that the local fire department is geared to prevent spread of fire rather than to extinguish it as soon as possible in the place of its origin. Furthermore, premiums applicable to highly protected property might include assessments designed to transfer to the owners the losses incurred by the insurers under laws requiring them to cover property they would prefer to reject.

A construction feature which has been proved hazardous is modern design. Many industrial plants built during the fifties and sixties featured efficient conveyance of materials and work-in-process through production areas which were not divided by fire resistive partitions. Some of them have been destroyed swiftly by fire. The countries in which companies have paid most heavily for this design seem to have been Belgium, Denmark, Germany, France, Italy, Japan, the Netherlands, and the United Kingdom.

Another mode of modern construction which contributed to fire damage in those countries was the use in the fifties and sixties of plastic paneling, sheathing, and roofing. The temperatures at which some of those materials burn and the density of smoke and toxicity of fumes have greatly hampered fire fighters.[3] Moreover, some of the materials have ignited not as the result of contact with flame but through spontaneous heating.

In most countries, the high cost of structural steel has caused companies—affiliates of American corporations included—to employ

forms of construction other than steel frame. Thus the need to econo-
mize has spared some companies the costly consequences of fires in
buildings framed by steel which was not insulated against the high
temperatures of industrial fires. Steel girders sag under temperatures
in excess of 925°C, with resultant collapse of walls, floors, roofs, and
overhead conveyor lines. Structures supported by walls of stone,
brick, or concrete can withstand much higher temperatures without
collapsing. Because very little structural steel has been used in construction of buildings in Latin America and southern Europe, cave-ins
during fires are rare in those areas. Steel framing is more common in
the United States and Canada than elsewhere. However, it is widely
used in Belgium, Germany, and the United Kingdom, and large industrial fire losses involving collapse of structural steelwork occurred in
all three countries.

Two of the hazards indicated above will change appreciably during
the later seventies and early eighties. Increasingly, such fire-containing
devices as automatic extinguishers, roof vents, and fireproof curtains
are being installed. However, fires fed by oils, gases, or chemicals can
overwhelm any barriers if human errors or mechanical defects have
weakened them. Such fires in buildings lacking fire-resistive partitions
continue to threaten many affiliates.

The hazard inherent in combustible plastic building materials will
be diminished by use of substitutes for the plastics now being employed in new construction and in modernization. Among substitutes
are materials which foam rather than ignite, wood treated to retard
spread of fire, and insulated sheet steel.

Little or no change in the hazard inherent in framing buildings with
steel uprights and trusses is likely; the high costs of such construction
will continue to confine that hazard to a few countries. Insulating
steel girders and plates will become more common, but the methods
of doing so (spraying on asbestos coatings, attaching precast jackets,
and enclosing in poured concrete) have been widely known for decades and are not likely to be adopted universally during the next
several years.

Changes in Industrial Methods and Equipment

New kinds of equipment and new methods of operation adopted by
manufacturers during the sixties resulted in costly fires. In particular,
greater concentrations of high-value property led to large losses. Inflationary increases in value of equipment and output accounted for
some of the rises in values, of course, but other developments contributed substantially. Acquisition of exceedingly complicated machine

tools and other electronic equipment entailed huge increases in values. Commonly, new equipment was also highly compact, occupying space which formerly had been unused or freeing space for installation of other equipment. Thus, with reduction in the bulk of computers, a Belgian manufacturer converted a small basement area which had been used for storage of crates into a computer center. Upon purchase of a machine tool which performs dozens of milling operations, a German manufacturer installed other expensive, multi-purpose machines in the space formerly occupied by single-function milling machines.

Another factor in the increased concentration of values were changes in storage methods. At the beginning of the fifties, stockpiling to heights of thirty feet or more was rare in even the highly industrialized countries of northern Europe. By the opening of the seventies, many companies in numerous countries were using new warehouses and the lift trucks and storage pallets designed for piling to such heights. In the larger and higher warehouses, therefore, the quantities of stored goods in each square foot of storage area were two or three times greater than those of a few years earlier. With greater quantities, of course, came greater values.

While increased concentration of values has been especially common in Belgium, Germany, the United Kingdom, and Japan, it has occurred in all the countries considered here. High piling in Brazil has contributed to unprecedented losses in warehouse fires. Expanded computer centers in Italy, Mexico, the Philippines, and Spain expose affiliates to possibility of major losses even if fires do not spread beyond the small area of the centers.

Another form of operational change which has increased probabilities of fire loss is reduction in the number of employees tending machines. Automated equipment—especially that controlled by computers—is tended by fewer employees than were needed to operate the earlier machines. With the dispersal of employees, discovery of some fires has been delayed calamitously.

Fluids used in many industrial operations are so volatile and ignition of the gases so rapid that their burning resembles an explosion. This hazard, like the others above, occurs in direct relation to industrial advancement. By the beginning of the seventies, the countries in which it was particularly widespread were Belgium, Germany, Japan, Mexico, the Netherlands, and the United Kingdom.

During the late seventies and early eighties, the hazards described in this section will continue to threaten affiliates of American companies. Probably, however, they will not become increasingly troublesome in countries where they have been long established. But they will emerge as problems in southern Europe and Latin America (other than Mexico).

Conditions Affecting Fire Control

Water Supplies and Pressures

The quantity of water which public systems provide for fighting fires and the water pressure available for attacking fires vary greatly within the United States. In many other countries, differences are less pronounced. Typically, water supplies are inadequate for fighting major fires inasmuch as they are scarcely sufficient for drinking, sanitation, washing, irrigation, and manufacturing. Pressures are insufficient for casting water fifty feet or more into burning buildings.[4] In such countries, firemen cannot be expected to bring all fires quickly under control.

Handicapping firefighters in many overseas areas are inadequate rainfall, long distances from rivers and bodies of water, scarcity of hydrants, and pipelines intended for the small-scale industrial operations of decades ago. Other areas have ample supplies of water but use delivery systems which are obsolete in terms of pressures, diameters of mains, or availability of hydrants. Spain's largest cities are in the first category and frequently impose restrictions on water usage. When fires occur during nights in which water flows have been reduced, fire fighters may be helpless. Mexico City is typical of the second category. Like many cities throughout Latin America, it lacks hydrants. In sections of the city where hydrants are widely spaced or nonexistent, firemen sometimes draw water from sumps built for that purpose. With good fortune, they bring fires under control before they drain the pits. In the many areas in which sumps are not available, they rely upon the contents of the tanks in their trucks.[5] Often, they cannot extinguish fires before the tanks run dry and watch helplessly as the flames consume property.

An even more common deficiency is pipeline diameter which is too small to be used with automatic sprinkler systems or hose lines. Corporate planners in the United States have proposed installing automatic sprinklers in new plants overseas only to learn that the plants were to be supplied via mains much too small for the systems to be effective.

In summary, throughout Latin America and in many localities elsewhere, industrial plants or large stores must augment public water supplies if they are to control fires. A company may be able to do so by sinking a well or laying a pipeline. It may have to construct tanks or a storage lagoon. If it is fortunate, it needs only to install pumps for boosting the pressure of water delivered by public mains.

Cities which entered the seventies equipped with water systems which were inadequate for fighting large fires are not likely to make major improvements before the end of the century. Replacing obsolete water delivery facilities is so costly that governments undertake it only when the primary need is for vast increases in water for drinking and sanitation.

Equipment

Equipment used by public fire departments throughout Europe, Japan, and Australia varies in quality much as in the United States. In the very large cities, the vehicles, pumps, hose lines, nozzles, ladders, lifts, and dispensers of chemicals suffice for the control of almost all fires.[6] In small and medium-sized cities, however, great variances occur. Some fire departments are as well equipped as those of any of the very large cities; some are essentially without equipment. Exceptions are the Republic of the Philippines and Spain, where small cities uniformly lack the means to combat large industrial fires.

Throughout Latin America, fire departments in only the largest cities are well equipped. Those in all other localities—including suburbs of the major cities—are outfitted in accordance with the continent-wide belief that fire is an insignificant peril.

Extensive equipping of commercial and industrial buildings with fire control facilities has been more common in the United States and Canada than elsewhere. Throughout Europe and Latin America, most buildings have only such items as standpipes, hose carts, and hand-held extinguishers. The main exceptions are buildings owned by United States-based companies, but many affiliates occupy buildings which have have only rudimentary internal protection.[7] The effectiveness of automatic sprinklers is recognized everywhere. However, the nationals who manage many affiliates of American corporations have been less impressed by the benefits of sprinkler systems than by the high costs of installation and the small reductions in fire insurance premiums they earn. Similarly, they have not applauded proposals to acquire private water supplies, water pressure boosters, systems for issuing carbon dioxide or foam, fire sensors, or fire control vehicles.

However, in all countries, municipalities and private companies improved their facilities during the seventies. The companies have moved farther and faster, having been alarmed by calamitous fires in buildings similar to their own. Moreover, the American owners of some companies forced local managers to install fire protection equipment in new and old buildings despite the managers' unhappiness with the expenditures.

Personnel

Everywhere those who fight fires admire expertise. Even men who otherwise have little interest either in learning or in cooperating study the chemistry and physics of fire and are proud of the teamwork with which their crews attack fires. Throughout the countries in which United States-based companies have affiliates, public fire departments are staffed by men who are well trained and diligent. Not all of them are qualified to attack infernos in oil refineries or chemical plants, but almost all are prepared to fight any other industrial fires.

Full-time members of companies' fire brigades are characterized by skill and intense interest in fire control. Brigade members whose main duties are unrelated to fire fighting also possess those traits.

While fire losses overseas seldom can be attributed to lack of able firemen, many are due to shortages of two other kinds of technicians, i.e., employees who specialize in preventing fires on their employers' premises, and consultants in fire prevention. The shortages result from lack of managerial interest in prevention; with very little demand for such specialists, few persons prepare themselves for careers in those fields.

In company fire prevention programs in the United States and Canada, employee specialists are engaged in research, analysis, education, and enforcement. Foreign affiliates which do not assign employees to those functions cannot profit from systematic study of fires incurred by other companies and do not build prevention measures into new construction or modernization.

Companies in the United States and Canada can hire consulting engineers to help them prevent fires, and they can use the services of fire prevention engineers employed by their insurance companies and brokers. Until the middle sixties the services of such specialists were available only in those European countries in which American insurers and brokers were doing large volumes of business. Domestic insurers in those countries continued to believe that risk bearing did not include casualty prevention. By the mid-seventies, however, they were beginning to compete with American insurers; one, indeed, sold prevention about as aggressively as insurance.

The mid-seventies also found American insurers and brokers lead-
ing reluctant domestic insurers in Australia, Japan, and the Republic
of the Philippines into providing small amounts of assistance in fire
prevention. Throughout Latin America, however, domestic carriers
continued to regard prevention as the responsibility of the policyholder alone. Moreover, because governments throughout Latin
America had taken steps during the sixties to reduce greatly the influence of foreign-controlled insurers, they virtually eliminated the possibility that competition provided by American insurers or brokers
would force domestic insurers to offer assistance in fire prevention.[8]

Consultants in fire prevention have been even less numerous outside the United States than prevention engineers employed by insurers and brokers. Managers who still are largely indifferent to the
availability of free prevention advice from insurers are not a lively
market for fee-charging consultants.

Since increasing numbers of European managers are accepting the
concept of comprehensive risk control and increasing numbers of
American owner corporations are moving to supervise closely the risk
control operations of their European affiliates, employment of fire
prevention specialists by large affiliates probably will be commonplace by the mid-eighties. That development probably will not cause
insurers or brokers to employ fewer prevention engineers, for managers who regard casualty prevention as the primary risk control
function will seek the experience and judgment of both outsiders and
employees.

In countries other than those of Europe and North America, the
numbers of fire prevention specialists available probably will be no
greater in 1985 than in 1975. Nationalism will bar American-controlled
insurers from furnishing fire prevention services superior to the negligible assistance provided by domestic insurers, and local managers
will continue to resist the urging of their owner corporations to employ full-time prevention specialists.

Customs

A variety of attitudes and practices—some local, some international—hamper fire fighters. The almost universal restriction on fire
departments against summoning help from other municipalities is an
example of the problem. Unless a fire department's chief requests
help, other departments cannot respond. Consequently, the owner of
a burning building calls only the local fire department, even though he
needs all the firemen and the apparatus of a half-dozen districts

immediately. While the restriction probably is necessary, it has resulted in total losses when the fire chiefs, whether from faulty judgment or false pride, delayed calling for help.[9]

In Brazil and to lesser degrees elsewhere in Latin America, fire departments assist police and military forces in curbing disorders; with powerful streams of water from their hose lines, firemen have quickly dispersed rioters. However effective it is as a means of mob control, the practice creates the possibility that firemen will be hosing mobs while property burns. Therefore two questions of priorities beset managers in such countries. If a fire department is called to deal simultaneously with a mob and a fire unrelated to the mob action, to which emergency will it respond? If the mob is both setting fires in stores and threatening to charge the jail in order to release political prisoners, will the fire crews first fight the fires or first break up the mass of persons surrounding the jail?

A standard tactic in fire fighting is to concentrate on containing the spread of fires. In general it is sound, preventing the huge losses in lives and money resulting from runaway fires. However, throughout Latin America and innumerable localities elsewhere in which equipment for fighting fires is inadequate, containment usually entails sacrificing the properties in which the fires began. Therefore, the owner of a building from which the fire might spread to nearby structures faces the possibility that public fire fighters will regard saving his property as a secondary objective. Long-established practices rarely are abandoned abruptly. An owner in that circumstance, therefore, must depend upon his own means of controlling fires. He must maintain a trained fire brigade and an automatic sprinkler system which would cool quickly the hottest fire which could occur on the premises.

Attitudes and Behavior of Rank-and-File Employees

A complaint which was raised widely by industry in the mid-sixties and had not faded by the mid-seventies was that various mixes of indifference and arrogance in young employees had made management a more difficult art than ever before. Indeed, some managers were fearful that those attitudes would not diminish with the maturing of a single, troubled generation but were so deeply ingrained that they would corrupt generations to follow. Particularly afflicted, seemingly, were young adults in nothern Europe. These two attitudes caused fires in commercial and industrial properties by such forms of misbehavior as violation of smoking regulations, haphazard maintenance of machines, ignorning instructions for the use of electrical equipment and the handling of combustible materials, and careless operation of plant vehicles.[10] Explosive spread of fire resulted from procrastination in disposal of inflammable wastes and from spilling fuels, lubricants, and other flammable fluids.

Throughout northern Europe, growth of these troublesome attitudes usually is attributed to decades of prosperity. If that diagnosis is accurate and if the attitudes persist, companies in countries in which young persons view prosperity as a permanent condition will bear a cost in the form of fires. Affiliates of United States-based corporations throughout Europe and in Australia, Japan, and Venezuela are likely to incur such losses into the eighties, at least.

Managerial Attitudes and Behavior

Apart from those directly responsible for preventing casualties, few persons in management in the United States find fire control a fascinating subject. Despite abundant evidence that prevention programs cannot be effective unless reinforced consistently by top management, many in management provide only grudging support. In comparison with their counterparts in other countries, however, managers in the United States are zealots in the cause of prevention. Except in Canada and (perhaps) Germany, managers abroad are almost totally uninterested. Consequently, in foreign affiliates of American companies managed by nationals who are unwilling to spend for fire control, the nationals' predictions of ineffectuality are self-fulfilling.

Among costly errors of affiliates' managers are refusal to discipline violators of smoking restrictions and other rules, refusal to hire prevention specialists, and vetoing proposals to build into new facilities such controls as automatic sprinkler systems, partitions for confining fires, breakaway outer walls for venting fiery blasts, and auxiliary water lines. Even if a plant manager is a prevention-minded American or an atypical national, his efforts to promote prevention tend to be smothered by the disbelief of department managers. Ordinarily, they can evade fire prevention responsibilities with impunity.

Only in the European countries considered here is significant improvement in managerial attitudes toward fire prevention likely during the seventies or early eighties.

Economic Conditions

Most foreign affiliates of American corporations are not in dire need of capital. However, many of the affiliates' domestic suppliers may be thus handicapped. If earnings have been low, banks are unwilling to lend, and investors are not interested in buying new issues of capital stock. Indeed, investors may ignore opportunities to buy stock in prospering companies.[11] In consequence of its inability to secure capital, a company may be forced to operate with worn equipment, cramped production and storage areas, inadequate water pressure, battered electrical systems, and other impaired facilities which can result in disastrous fires.

An affiliate dependent upon an undercapitalized supplier faces a high probability of loss if fire ravages the supplier's plant; quite likely, the supplier will not be able to ship sufficient parts from inventory to permit the affiliate to produce without interruption of operations. Consequently, the affiliate will have to set up facilities for producing the parts or arrange for another company to make them. Either adjustment requires increased spending, and its suspension of production could be costly.

Another economic situation which creates fire hazards is prolonged operation at maximum levels of production. A foreign affiliate may overuse its machines and personnel for several consecutive years in its desire to take full advantage of opportunity to produce large earnings. In so doing, the affiliate postpones overhauls of equipment and takes shortcuts in routine maintenance. Such neglect results in overheating, leakage, and undetected wear. At least as dangerous as failure to repair or replace worn parts of equipment is failure to relieve exhaustion which drains employees of alertness and concentration. Whether fatigue besets machines or employees, fire may result.

NOTES

1. Fractures vary in length from a few hundred feet to several hundred miles. Some have occurred at the earth's surface, while others have been as much as 400 miles beneath it. The longer a fracture and the closer to the surface, the more drastically it reshapes the surface by fissuring and thrusting up or depressing rock and soil and the more violent is the shuddering of the crust. Most damage is caused by the quaking motion resulting from energy release. Occasionally, however, surface distortion directly above a fracture topples buildings or tears roads.
2. While fracturing releases energy, it does not eliminate the conditions behind the pressures. (Geologists differ in their identification of the conditions.)
3. Damage to computers by corrosive fumes emitted by burning plastic paneling has been an unusual and costly form of loss.
4. A flow of 6,000 gallons per minute per section of a burning building used for metal-cutting operations at a pressure of fifty pounds per square inch ordinarily

suffices for control of such a fire; 24-inch water mains and pressures of thirty pounds will permit control of almost any ground-level fire in an industrial plant. Even 12-inch mains will provide adequate water for fighting such fires if pressure is at least fifty pounds.

5. While a pumper might deliver 10,000 gallons of water, that quantity might be only a fraction of the amount needed to extinguish a major fire.

6. An exception is fire in upper stories of high-rise buildings. Such structures now are numerous throughout Europe, Latin America, and elsewhere. As in the United States, firemen are severely handicapped in fighting fires high above street levels.

7. The author visited a modern plant in England owned by an American corporation in which the fire-fighting equipment consisted of water buckets.

8. By 1970, insurance regulators throughout the continent were discouraging fire prevention engineers based in the United States from even brief tours of industrial plants of affiliates of American corporations.

9. Management of a company located in a small town, therefore, must learn how the local chief would react to need of help from other towns. If it finds that he probably would hesitate to ask assistance, it must either impress him with evidence that a fire on its premises would spread with exceptional speed, or—if he is uneducable— add to its facilities for fighting fires.

10. In sharp contrast is the regard for machines by Mexican employees of all ages. They operate machines with care and watch closely for indications of need of repairs or readjustments.

11. The French, for example, prefer to place their money in real estate in times of prosperity and in gold during recessions.

6

CASUALTY PREVENTION SYSTEMS

Examined in this chapter are structural and financial foundations of casualty prevention programs in foreign affiliates, problems of those who work to prevent casualties, and patterns of responsibility necessary for coping with the problems. The areas of prevention considered are job-caused injuries to employees, damage to the bodies and property of customers or other outsiders, damage by fire or explosion to company property, and thefts by employees or others.

Foundations of Programs of Prevention

Establishing Objectives

Formal recognition of objectives is as necessary in casualty prevention abroad as in any other corporate activity. The broad purposes of risk control indicated in Chapter 1 (i.e., protecting of profit margins, increasing of profit margins, and preventing of severe financial dislocations through sudden reduction in assets) are not adequate as casualty prevention objectives for those working to prevent casualties in foreign affiliates. Needed instead are specifics which are demanding but clearly attainable. To control embezzlement in a manufacturer's branch operation in Britain, for example, the objectives might include these:

> Reduction of loss of tools and output through employee pilferage (as indicated by otherwise inexplicable shortages and disappearances) from the annual levels during the past four years of 5–9 percent of cost of goods produced to 3 percent.

> Development and adjustment of a system for testing computer procedures applicable to purchasing, shipping, receiving, payroll, employee benefits, and cash accounts in order to detect embezzlements by computer personnel within five days of commencement.

If such objectives are to spur employees, they must be established by management. Directors of risk control and employees specializing in fire prevention, accident prevention, plant security, and embezzlement control can provide technical assistance, but they are not experienced in setting objectives which exert pressure and at the same time present an opportunity to demonstrate abilities. Unfortunately for many companies in every country, those in top management feel little enthusiasm for creating casualty prevention objectives. The disinterest is more pronounced elsewhere than in the United States, conventional opinion holding that management should leave defensive activities such as risk control entirely to subordinates. Consequently, nationals managing affiliates abroad which are essentially autonomous in casualty prevention might not establish useful objectives. If feasible under such circumstances, top management of the owner corporation sets the objectives and requires local management to evaluate its performance in prevention in the light of those objectives.

Budgeting for Prevention

Management cannot establish objectives without deciding upon the limits to expenditures. The latter is the more difficult aspect of prevention. Management knows that an unlimited capacity to pay for prevention programs would assure a negligible incidence of casualties. It knows also, however, that it cannot authorize unlimited spending and that the company's specialists therefore must work toward goals considerably short of complete prevention.

In the short run, setting unduly low limits on expenditures for the various prevention programs may not be detrimental inasmuch as insurance recoveries may compensate for losses. Eventually, however, insurance costs will reflect the large amounts of loss which result from spending little on prevention. And if a company spends minimally on both insurance and prevention, its out-of-pocket losses eventually may be disastrous. Therefore, decision making as to expenditures for casualty prevention must include anticipation of the high costs to be experienced sooner or later if the company is to spend only token amounts.

These are the chief guidelines commonly employed in such decision making.

Costs of preventive programs should not exceed the value of the resultant benefits, i.e., reduction in losses.

In keeping with the principle of diminishing returns, periodic increases in expenditures for prevention eventually will no longer produce proportionate additional savings.

Management's humaneness or governmental pressure may require that preventive programs which might save employees from injuries have budgetary priority over programs aimed solely at protecting the company against loss of income or assets. Therefore, if spending for prevention for the coming year must be lower than that for the current year, the saving must be accomplished by pruning expenditures for control of such perils as embezzlement or damage to products in transit. Spending for fire prevention and employee accident prevention probably cannot be cut.

The first two are statements of the same principle from different viewpoints. They rest upon logic, but management ordinarily pays only lip service to them. It knows that it cannot measure the value of casualty losses avoided last year through preventive effort, inasmuch as chance, too, was a determinant—to an unknown extent. Consequently, it spends little time in attempting to calculate the results of spending on prevention during the coming year, budgeting instead by guessing.

Except as a reminder to place first things first, the third consideration, too, is of little budgetary value. For example, if top management has ordered a 25 percent reduction in spending for prevention for the coming year and the director of risk control believes that expenditures for preventing fires, explosions, and on-the-job accidents must not be reduced, he must apportion the reduction over the other preventive programs. Because he cannot predict the impacts of reduced spending on the other programs, he apportions arbitrarily. Inasmuch as he feels that (a) burglary loss will not be very large even if the amount to be spent on burglary prevention is greatly reduced and (b) loss through products liability claims could be so large that he must spend every available penny on preventing the marketing of faulty products, he apportions accordingly.

Eventually directors of risk control may base their requests for spending on casualty prevention on estimated benefits and costs over periods long enough to distinguish between the impacts of preventive efforts and chance. Ideally they will do so in response to corporate policy requiring that the risk control function contribute to measurable portions of profits. Top managers of their companies will compare debits and credits related to risk control over periods of five or six years, expecting expenditures to produce substantial margins of credits over debits.[1] Under such accountability, prevention programs will be expected to produce specified amounts of savings—again, probably, over five- or six-year periods.

Problems in Casualty Prevention

Fragmented Handling of Risk

Companies which have not centralized the risk control function in their domestic operations are ill-equipped to oversee casualty prevention abroad. They lack managers who are able to supervise casualty prevention by remote control and have observed successes and failures of programs under wide varieties of conditions. Moreover such companies lack the breadth of experience necessary for evaluation of performance in prevention.

Under these conditions, top management of an owner corporation can hope only that a few of the affiliates will work effectively to prevent casualties. The majority of the affiliates will not even resent lack of guidance by the owner. In their assumption that prevention is not a significant function of management, they will be content with making sporadic gestures toward prevention.

Divided supervision of casualty prevention also occurs when American owner corporations oversee the function in some of their affiliates while deferring in others to co-owners desirous of supervising it. The programs controlled by the American owners may be fully as effective as those of their units in the United States. Those supervised by the co-owners may be worthless.

Unsuccessful programs can contribute to devastating net losses. Therefore, if top management of an American corporation has no control over casualty prevention in a jointly owned affiliate and knows that the programs are ineffectual, it has a duty to take corrective action. Unless it foresees improvements in sales or cost control so great as to make failures in casualty prevention meaningless, it must move to improve the programs or recommend that the interest in the affiliate be sold.

Problems in Prevention Education

Unless the owner corporation's management regards casualty prevention as a necessity, it does not put pressure on managers of foreign affiliates to maintain effective programs. Unless the owner corporation's director of risk control motivates top management, it does not apply such pressure. Moreover, unless the director of risk control assists the affiliates' managers—whether or not they are under such direction by top management—they probably will not create useful programs.

Unfortunately for the shareholders of many owner corporations, the corporate directors of risk control are not responsible for educating either top management in the ever increasing need for preventing casualties or the affiliates' managers in administering programs of prevention. Many corporate directors of risk control, in fact, have no responsibilities in prevention at home or abroad. Others, according to their job descriptions, are responsible for educating management in risk control but in actuality do not have access to management of either the owner corporations or the affiliates.

Furthermore, even if an owner corporation's director of risk control is responsible for guiding local managers in prevention and is authorized to communicate with them, he encounters frustration. Coupled with the slowness of the process of chipping away at managerial disinterest in prevention is the manager's belief that advice given by the owner corporation's employees probably is academic verbiage based upon superficial knowledge of local hazards. If the affiliate employs specialists in casualty prevention, efforts of the corporate director of risk control and his associates to contribute to their education may be futile; the specialists will not learn much from those they regard as theoreticians worthy of minimal attention. If an affiliate employs no specialists, the director of risk control may have to work directly with the department heads who must enforce prevention regulations. His main problem may be their belief that the programs are exercises for the purpose of demonstrating top management's determination to protect the interests of the stockholders. Their subordinates recognize their cynicism and react in the predictable manner.

Problems in Obtaining Information

Without close knowledge of hazards, those charged with preventing casualties can accomplish little. Obviously, owner corporations' directors of risk control and specialists in prevention cannot possess complete information on affiliates' hazards. Even in domestic operations, changes in methods of production, personnel, products, environmental conditions, and locations of facilities create changes in hazards. And however diligently such changes are searched out, only the occurrence of casualties will reveal many of them. Difficulties in gathering information relating to hazards abroad are even more formidable. Owner corporations can readily obtain reports on changes in laws and on causes of damage to property and injuries to people. Except in Canada and the United Kingdom, however, they cannot tap flows of risk-related news like that provided in the United States by such media as technical journals, research monographs, government publications, subscription services, and releases by professional and industry associations. Furthermore, they are prevented by distance, language, and laxity from obtaining prompt notification by their affiliates of changes in hazards.

International insurance brokers provide clients with information on hazards in countries in which they maintain offices or are associated with domestic brokers. Ordinarily, however, they are better fitted to provide background information on nationwide changes and predictions of economic or legal changes than to uncover happenings within individual companies. They sometimes astonish owner corporations with their knowledge of developments within the affiliates, but they cannot secure all the facts on all changes in the companies' hazards.

Useful to some directors of risk control are recollections of employees who have returned from assignments in foreign affiliates. Even if the returnees are not particularly concerned with hazards in their work, some have learned of conditions of interest to risk controllers. Ideally, the director of risk control or an associate talks with each returnee. Unfortunately, many of those who have been abroad are too busy wrestling with problems which accumulated during their visits to search their memories for items related to hazards. Also barring directors of risk control from this source of information is top management's failure to require that returnees submit to interviewing.

The risk controller's most effective means of keeping abreast of changes in affiliates' hazards is combining periodic, on-premises discussions with telephone talks. If he is to help the affiliates detect changes in hazards and is to induce them to keep him informed he must spend time every year or two on their premises. Between the meetings, he continues to communicate by telephone and mail.

Commonly, top management does not believe that the benefits of periodic meetings of the director of risk control and overseas managers are worth the costs. Knowing that a system of control of any kind must be based upon knowledge, its refusal to support continuous search for changes in hazards reflects its belief that casualty prevention cannot be productive.

Problems in Employing U.S. Practices Abroad

Often a practice which has prevented casualties in the United States is also effective abroad. Because it may be unaware of some hazards, however, management cannot assume that exporting its practices will be successful. Illustrative is a corporation's requirement in its domestic operations that maintenance employees wear face masks while spraying-painting indoors. The rule has been enforced consistently and probably has been the main reason that maintenance workers have reported no respiratory damage during the past twenty years. Management, therefore, has instructed each of the foreign affiliates to protect its painters in that manner. Unfortunately, it will be disappointed. It is unaware of the contempt with which rank-and-file employees in several of the affiliates regard recommendations of the owner corporation and of the fatalistic belief of managers in some of the units that employee injuries are, inevitably, a sizeable part of the cost of production. Consequently, the affiliates' painters do not wear masks, certain that they will not be disciplined, and regularly inhale particles of paint and enamel.

Another barrier to employing successfully abroad the preventive measures which are used in the United States is lack of effective local administrators. Almost any preventive technique must be adapted to such local peculiarities as employee illiteracy and inability to understand instructions, animosity within management, interference of labor unions or local governments, long waits for special equipment, and oddities of buildings. Moreover, changes in conditions within an affiliate's plant may require periodic modification of preventive techniques. The changes might be among the following: damage to facilities, strikes, hiring of new supervisors, and conversion of production by governmental order, to name a few such changes. Employees of owner corporations can assist in adapting to local needs the methods developed in the United States, but qualified local specialists are essential. Commonly, however, affiliates do without them, determined to avoid investing in training or hiring of experienced practitioners.

Responsibilities in Casualty Prevention

Responsibilities of Owner Corporation's Director of Risk Control and of Casualty Prevention Specialists

Most of the United States-based corporations which operate extensively abroad do not make their risk controllers responsible for affiliates' efforts to prevent casualties. The patterns of responsibility indicated below, therefore, are those followed by the owner corporations which stand apart from the majority in their belief that their prevention personnel can help affiliates increase their earnings by avoiding casualties.

The risk controllers' responsibility which is most beneficial to many affiliates is that of answering questions asked by the administrators of their programs. Whether inexperienced or expert, the administrators frequently need information, opinions, and reassurance. The conscientious corporate director of risk control obtains answers, often at the considerable cost of talking with persons in several countries. With such reinforcement, affiliates' employees are reminded that the owner corporation's management is certain that the benefits of casualty prevention are worth substantial spending.

A related responsibility is providing advice to affiliates which are to build new facilities, move to new locations, renovate property, introduce new products, or enter new markets. If the director of risk control causes managers to include facilities for minimizing fire damage, discouraging theft, preventing on-the-job injuries and injuries to customers, they contribute to the avoidance of casualties at minimal costs.

The responsibility which is most frequently overlooked, probably, is that of sustaining awareness of the need to watch continuously for changes in hazards. Although the difficulties in obtaining information on such changes are formidable barriers to the timely adjustment of prevention programs, the greatest obstruction of all is overlooking the inevitability of changes in hazards. The management which is appreciative of the worth of casualty prevention does not fail to adjust, for example, to the discovery that it is releasing into the atmosphere carcinogenic agents in a gaseous waste. If it is not endlessly alert to the possibility of old or new hazards, it cannot make the moves which will prevent the hazards from maturing into casualties.

Responsibilities of Owner Corporation's Top Management

The chief responsibility of corporate top management in casualty prevention abroad is to establish objectives for the guidance of local managers. Ideally, in order to meet the objectives, local management sets one or more secondary objectives. Thus, corporate management demands that "eventually" the number of lost-time injuries in iron foundries must be brought to a figure 15 percent below the averages of the affiliates' countries. And thus, an affiliate moves toward that objective via intermediate objectives. One is the reducing of the company's accident rate in its foundry to a level equal to the national average in no more than three years. The other is to lower the rate to the 85 percent level in no more than four additional years.

Similarly, corporate management's decree that supervisors be trained to regard the prevention of pilferage by rank-and-file employees as one of their daily responsibilities leads to a sub-objective: within three months, supervisors and management are to develop open-end lists of acts or aspects of appearance of workers in the various occupational areas which should be regarded as indicators of pilfering.

Another responsibility of corporate management is the applying of pressure on affiliates' managers to spend the amounts of money necessary for successful prevention. Even if top management permits managers abroad to develop their own budgets, it must make clear that the amounts budgeted for the various areas of prevention are realistic, not mere gestures.

Responsibilities of Affiliate's Management

In addition to achieving objectives established by the owner corporation, the affiliate's management is responsible for assigning full-time and part-time duties in prevention and for arranging the training of employees in their duties. Much of the training occurs on the employer's premises and is inexpensive, but some of it is costly. A former member of the city's fire department who is to be in charge of fire control may need considerable training in the engineering involved in providing sufficient quantities of water to control industrial fires via automatic sprinklers and hose lines. When the training entails importing instructors or sending employees to other countries for months, local management is responsible for meeting the substantial costs.

Evaluating performance is another responsiblity of the affiliate's management. Even though it cannot measure closely the savings achieved through the preventive efforts of individual employees, it must make estimates. Probably it can do so by comparing the affiliate's casualties over periods of several years with those of other companies.

NOTES

1. Credits, presumably, will include values of assets preserved through prevention of casualties, estimated gains derived by preventing reduction in flows of revenues, and anticipated values of clearing barriers to moving successfully into new products, processes, territories, and affiliations. Debits will include costs of casualty prevention programs, insurance, absorbed casualty losses, and salaries of risk control personnel.

7

GOVERNMENT-CAUSED PROBLEMS IN INSURING FOREIGN OPERATIONS

In any insurance market, users of insurance encounter problems caused by the attitudes, customs, and financial conditions of their protectors. They also encounter problems created by those who prescribe insurance regulations and those who enforce them. This chapter identifies problems of the latter category and considers the prospects for finding solutions.

Nationalism

Examined below are controls which governments impose upon selling and buying insurance in order to exclude foreign capital and personnel from domestic insurance markets and thus promote national prosperity and self-esteem.

Manifestations

In an extreme form, nationalism in insurance is governmental operation of an insurance monopoly. By the opening of the seventies, most of the twenty-five emerging nations in Africa seemed to be headed in that direction, tolerating the presence of foreign-owned insurers temporarily while hoping that government-owned carriers soon would be sufficiently large and experienced to permit expulsion of the foreigners. They intended, of course, that insurance profits thereafter would be available for governmental use rather than go abroad to foreign owners.

Brazil, Chile, and Venezuela have established governmental monopolies in reinsurance in order to reduce flows of premiums to Europe and the United States. Under their systems, only portions of the largest and most unattractive risks are reinsured abroad. The approach entails (a) requiring each domestic insurer to obtain its reinsurance from the government's reinsurance pool, (b) the pool's apportioning each risk among the domestic companies, and (c) transferring to foreign insurers the portions of risks that exceed the capacities of the domestic companies. In Japan a government bureau is the exclusive reinsurer of companies selling compulsory auto insurance. The French government operates a reinsurance company which is not a monopolistic carrier but is entitled to write up to 4 percent of any reinsurance sought by private insurance companies.

In countries which long have had industrial economies, the most common product of nationalism in insurance is legislation requiring that insurance applicable to domestic business operations be purchased from home-owned insurers or from foreign insurers admitted to the domestic markets under licenses. Numerous countries combine this restriction with the policy of discouraging foreign insurers from seeking admission; their regulatory bureaus either refuse to license foreigners or do so grudgingly. Denmark and Japan are among countries employing this combination.

Ordinarily, a requirement that insurance be purchased in the domestic market does not bar going abroad for protection not available domestically; instead, laws permit companies which cannot meet their needs in their domestic markets to request permission to insure elsewhere. However, German law discourages such shopping abroad by imposing a pair of unusual requirements. One bars the use of agents or brokers in insuring operations in Germany under policies secured in foreign markets. Its effect is to make insuring in markets outside Germany impracticable except for corporations having employees abroad who can negotiate directly with prospective insurers. The other requires payment of German premium taxes on insurance applicable in Germany, even though the policyholders secured their protection abroad and already have paid the taxes imposed in those markets. Under such double taxation, insurance costs are inflated by as much as 30 percent.

Laws requiring insurance buyers to patronize domestic markets apply throughout the United States, in European countries other than the Netherlands and the United Kingdom, all Latin American countries, South Africa, and Japan.[1] In Europe their immediate purposes are to produce tax revenue and prevent outward flows of premiums. In Japan and throughout Latin America they are intended also to shield domestic insurance companies from foreign competition.

Protecting private reinsurance companies against competition from foreigners is unusual, presumably because of governmental approval of foreigners' participation in bearing large losses. Mexican law, however, requires that at least 50 percent of the reinsurance applicable to any fire risk be secured in the domestic market. Another exception is Japan, which demands that virtually all reinsurance of risks of loss by fire as well as perils unlikely to cause catastrophic losses be secured from Japanese insurers. Conversely, the government encourages domestic insurance companies to obtain all their reinsurance in foreign markets.

A widening manifestation of nationalism is the barring of foreign nationals from control of domestic insurance companies through ownership or presence in top management. While Japan and other countries long have barred foreigners from exercising much control over domestic companies, Latin American countries attempted to eliminate foreign influence entirely. Mexico led the way, responding in the mid-thirties to resentment engendered by aliens' domination of some of its most profitable companies. By inundating insurers with ambiguous regulations pertaining to pricing, investments, and reporting, it drove from the market numerous foreign-controlled companies and many aliens who had managed companies owned mainly by Mexicans. However, British, American, and other insurers continued to influence some companies which were nominally Mexican. Consequently, during the early sixties the government began pressuring such insurers to place managerial control in the hands of Mexican nationals. Thus, while foreigners can own stock in a domestic company, Mexicans must occupy the top echelon of management.

In 1964 Venezuela's legislature moved in a more direct manner than Mexico's to reduce foreign influence, requiring that at least 51 percent of the stock of any insurance company doing business in the domestic market be owned by Venezuelan nationals. Argentina, Costa Rica, Guatemala, Peru, and Uruguay also have moved to end dominance of their markets by foreign insurers.

Significance of Nationalistic Restrictions

Penalties

Governmental barriers to purchasing insurance outside domestic markets clearly have had adverse effects upon international insurers, agents, and brokers. An insurer which has not been admitted to a market can sell little or no insurance there. A broker who could best serve a client by placing the risk in a nonadmitted carrier faces the possibility that he will be fined and lose his license if he does so.

Of much greater significance to corporate users of insurance, however, is the fact that such laws also prescribe fines for insureds and (in a few countries) their officers.[2] Indeed, under Mexican law the courts can both fine and jail executives of companies which patronize nonadmitted insurers without governmental permission.

Tax codes of some countries stipulate punishment for corporations which by-pass domestic markets by use of insurance contracts applicable to their affiliates wherever located. Punishment under such codes may be considerably more costly than the penalties indicated above. Under capital gains taxes imposed by Italy and numerous other countries, affiliates' recoveries via "world-wide" policies can be taxed as increases in capitalization. Under the German premium tax rule outlined above, double taxation might eliminate the savings anticipated in buying "world-wide" coverage in markets in which premium taxes are negligible, e.g., the Netherlands, the United Kingdom, or several of the states in the United States. The feasibility of including German operations in "world-wide" coverage is further reduced by the German government's systematic comparison of initial (estimated) charges for the German affiliates' protection with the actual charges. If an actual charge proves to be lower than the estimate, the affiliate must pay income, operating profits, and capital gains taxes on the excess. The combined taxes will almost equal the difference in the charges and might be several times the premium tax which would have applied had the charges not differed.

Other complications in use of "world-wide" policies

Directors of risk control of many American corporations have much more confidence in protection under "world-wide" policies than in coverage of policies issued individually in the markets of affiliates' countries. Having negotiated a "world-wide" policy, a director of risk control knows the perils covered, amounts of protection, exclusions, conditions, and bases of measuring the insurer's liabilities in losses. He is confident that those provisions will apply wherever the affiliates operate. If he has been systematic and farsighted in his discussions with the insurer, he knows its interpretations of all significant clauses. He may have entered into oral agreements in the certainty that the insurer will honor them. He feels secure because the contract is in English.[3]

Another reason for his favoring the "world-wide" approach is expectation of savings. Premiums are lower, and the cost in time of negotiating with a single insurer which he has found to be trustworthy and informed is much lower than that spent negotiating individually in the affiliates' markets.

A director of risk control who finds such worth in "world-wide" plans of insurance resents being forced to insure each affiliate in the market of its country, particularly if his favorite insurers have not been admitted to those markets and the affiliates must insure with companies he regards as undercapitalized, inflexible, and directed by persons who regard payment of claims as an admission of lack of fortitude. While the affiliates may benefit from goodwill on the part of the domestic insurers, he doubts that such gain will outweigh the disadvantages.

Managerial unwillingness to meet those costs is quite common, and numerous companies therefore insure "world-wide," living with risk of censure and penalization. In effect, the owner corporation pretends either that its "world-wide" policy does not exist or that it does not apply to operations in the particular country. The affiliate buys in the domestic market the workmen's compensation, auto, or fire insurance which may be mandatory and impliedly uses no other forms. Quite likely it can appear to use few insurances without being conspicuous, for such covers as products liability, difference in conditions, manufacturer's output, business interruption, "all-risks," blanket fidelity, comprehensive crime, and officers' and directors' liability may be little used in its country. Moreover, if the owner corporation is determined to conceal its protection under a "world-wide" policy, it probably can do so indefinitely. It can camouflage the affiliate's contributions toward the policy's costs in payments for materials or services. It can transmit loss payments to the affiliate in association with other transfers of funds, such as additions to capital.

In some countries, such subterfuge is unnecessary; the governments discourage purchase of insurance abroad but concede that the realities of international business will cause many companies to circumvent the restrictions. Thus, while Italian law bans use of insurance purchased from nonadmitted insurers, realistic officials tolerate the open recovery in Italy of losses covered under owner corporations' "world-wide" policies.

The basic question confronting owner corporations which have affiliates in many countries, therefore, is not whether they can circumvent market restrictions and use "world-wide" policies but whether they choose to practice such evasion.

Dissatisfaction with insurance purchased under duress

Compliance with requirements that insurance be purchased only in domestic markets does not necessarily lead to dissatisfaction. Among the insurers in any market may be companies equipped with capital and talent sufficient to meet the most unusual of insurance needs. The presence of domestic and admitted alien insurers may generate enough competition to assure high levels of service and low premium rates.

Commonly, however, American directors of risk control are not content with the tight restrictions they encounter in overseas markets mainly because they are not certain that the protection is adequate. They are apprehensive about contracts written in languages other than English, their inability to obtain protection limits as high as desired, the possibility that insurers or reinsurers are undercapitalized, and the probability of delays in recovering losses. They are dissatisfied with markets lacking innovative and service-minded insurers. In such markets, premium rates tend to be rigid and unjustifiably high, premium taxes are high, and insurers respond reluctantly or not at all to customers' unusual needs.

Trends and Prospects

In forecasting changes in nationalistic restrictions upon insurance buying and their effects upon foreign operations of United States-based corporations, placement of countries in four categories is useful. Indicated below are trends in the late seventies and conditions likely to exist in the early eighties in member countries of the European Economic Community (the European Common Market), the newly emerged countries of Africa, Latin American nations, and others.

Members of European Economic Community

The significance to American owner corporations of insurance developments in the European Economic Community is treated mainly in the section "Regionalism" below. However, because an all-important objective of the common market movement is to remove nationalistic hindrance to economic activity within the region, consideration of the progress toward that objective is appropriate.

The Community's planners began urging during the early sixties that the members move toward "harmonization" of insurance regulation by removing two nationalistic restrictions upon alien insurers' selling insurance. One of the reforms would have enabled an insurer domiciled in any member country to do business in any of the others without having been licensed by them as an admitted foreigner. The other would have enabled an insurer domiciled outside the Community but admitted to the market of one of the member nations to provide insurance anywhere in the Community. If those proposals were to be implemented, an American owner corporation could insure an affiliate in whichever segment of the Community's market it preferred; if it chose to insure its German operations with a British insurer which did not maintain offices in Germany, it could do so without governmental interference. If it wished to insure its Belgian affiliate with an American company which had been admitted only to the Italian segment of the Community's market, it could negotiate freely with that insurer. And if it wished to cover all affiliates in member countries under a "world-wide" contract issued by the underwriters at Lloyd's, London, it could do so openly.

As the seventies moved toward their close, the progress of these proposals had been barely perceptible. In France and Italy, in particular, insurers domiciled in other member countries could write insurance only after being licensed as admitted aliens. American insurance companies which had been admitted to individual markets could not transact business freely throughout the Community without obtaining licenses from the other members.

Clearly, two decades of discussion and voting had not eliminated nationalism as an economic force in Europe's insurance market.

Newly emerged countries

In the opinion of some European observers, nationalistic fervor and belief in state ownership as the quickest route to national prosperity will continue through the eighties to move the newly emerged nations of Africa toward eviction of all representatives of foreign insurers. Observers predict delays in the takeovers of the markets by monopolistic, government-owned insurers because officials are aware that a consequence would be the charging of unbearable reinsurance rates by foreign insurers. However, pan-African reinsurance facilities may be developed eventually, with consequent removal of influence of even foreign reinsurers.

By the mid-eighties, laws of the emerging nations requiring that insurance be purchased only in domestic markets may be enforced with such nationalistic vigor that foreign companies will not attempt evasion through use of "world-wide" or other policies written abroad.

Latin American countries

Because of the decades of resentment engendered in all Latin American countries by foreign insurers' aggressive and profitable performance in their markets, nationalism is likely to be a force in these markets indefinitely. However, governmental desire in most of the countries to eliminate need of foreign capital in their markets probably will not be realized by the mid-eighties; large amounts of capital will be needed in other areas of the economies, and expansion of domestic insurance facilities probably will have low priorities.

Effort to force corporations to insure in domestic markets will be intensified, and by the mid-eighties illicit purchasing of protection in American and European markets may be unusual. Paradoxically, the shielding of domestic insurers from competition from foreigners may lead to a resolution of the conflict in purposes between restrictive governments and would-be users of "world-wide" policies. The means may be a variation of a Venezuelan idea, whereby the issuer of a "world-wide" policy would invite participation by insurers in the countries in which affiliates were to be covered.[4] Each participating insurer would share in premiums and losses on a proportionate basis. In an international marketplace such as the Amsterdam-Rotterdam Bourse, commitment of insurers of numerous countries to such participation could be arranged quickly and economically.[5]

Other countries

In countries which are not in any of the three groups indicated above, governments are not likely to become either more or less restrictive by the mid-eighties. With the exception of Japan, nationalism has not greatly affected their insurance markets. The Japanese national government has long required that companies operating in the country insure primarily with domestic insurers and is unlikely to permit foreign insurers to write substantial volumes of business in the near future.

Impacts upon use of captive insurance companies

A corporate practice which will be affected by nationalism during the eighties is use of captive insurance companies. Corporations organized the earliest captives solely to cover their United States-based operations, but during the sixties some began establishing captives for protecting their foreign operations. The latter development has not been commonplace, and governments have hesitated to declare that use of foreign captives is equivalent to insuring with nonadmitted companies. However, if such use of captives expands, governments which are particularly zealous in protecting domestic insurers will rule that insuring with foreign captives is illegal.

Few captives, if any, will seek admitted status, for their value derives in part from minimal regulation. Consequently, even though a corporation's use of a captive is merely an elaborate means of absorbing its losses systematically, Latin American and African countries probably will move to prevent the use of captives in lieu of insuring in their markets. European governments might not do so for several reasons. One reason is their awareness that captives buy large amounts of reinsurance from European insurers. Another is belief that levying special taxes upon insurance provided by captives, to compensate for by-passed premium taxes, might be preferable to ousting foreign captives. Still another is the possibility that domestic corporations will want to employ captives to insure their affiliates in the United States and will need reciprocal tolerance on the part of state insurance departments.

In countries such as Japan, where the usual mode of investment by foreigners is the joint venture, governments probably will not have to rule on the legality of jointly owned companies' use of captives owned by the American partners, for the American co-owners are not likely to demand that their captives insure the companies.

Regionalism

Owner corporations operating in Europe and Latin America wrestle not only with problems generated by nationalism but also with difficulties created by a new form of regionalism—the common market movements. In the early seventies, the movements began to affect insurance markets.

European Economic Community

Many American directors of risk control expect establishment by the European Economic Community of a multi-national insurance market to result in substantial improvements in protection and cost. Others, however, fear that this pioneer effort will subject them to uncertainties for many years.

Objectives

Insurance objectives are minor purposes of the European Economic Community. To American corporations having affiliates in the region, however, they are important. The fundamental intention, with regard to insurance, is to restructure insurance facilities in order to maximize the industry's contribution to the prosperity of the member countries. The planners believe that the means thereto is an integrated market. They view integration not as a merging of insurance companies but as the bringing about of (a) ready access of insurance buyers to sellers located anywhere in the region, and (b) uniformity in the regulation of insurers.

Thus the Council of Ministers has asked the members to grant insurance companies domiciled in any of the countries the same right to transact business within their borders that they afford their domestic insurers. A company domiciled in Italy, that is, would face no legal handicaps in competing in Oslo with Norwegian insurers. And thus the Council's Commission strives to "harmonize" members' insurance regulatory laws and enforcement practices.

Barriers

The original appointees to the Commission achieved "harmonization" of the financial standards to be met by insurers, but their successors have moved very slowly on the issue of extent of governmental control to be exercised over policy provisions and premium rates. Their adoption, in effect, of a goal of partial "harmonization" in that area for the indefinite future was predictable for three reasons. The first is a habitual international suspicion. Delegates of one country automatically assume that a proposal of representatives of another is designed to increase earnings of insurers in the proponents' country at the expense of insurers elsewhere.

The second is a wide array of patterns of regulation of insurers. For instance, government in the United Kingdom exercises a negligible amount of control over Lloyd's operations, whereas French and German governments control domestic carriers tightly. The commissioners recognized that they could not soon establish a middle ground between the two approaches. Other important regulatory differences reflect fundamental differences in objectives underlying regulatory practices. In the Netherlands and the United Kingdom regulation is intended—almost exclusively—to maintain insurers' solvency by prescribing financial standards and monitoring financial condition. In the other member countries, it is directed also toward protection of policyholders against insurers' ineptitude and annoying practices: regulators oversee the drafting of policy forms and clauses and the calculating of premiums as well as the conducting of audits. Because Dutch and British insurers have prospered under liberal regulation and their policyholders have been reasonably content, Dutch and British appointees to the Commission have opposed proposals of conversion to the more comprehensive systems. Conversely, representatives of the other countries have insisted that comprehensive regulation is necessary.

The third reason for settling for partial harmonization are differences in two areas of law: taxation of premium income of insurers and defining legal liability. Some of the member countries view premium taxation as a means of raising revenue for general purposes, France and Italy being particularly dependent upon it. Belgium, Germany, and Luxembourg collect only small excesses over their costs of insurance regulation, and Ireland, the Netherlands, Norway, and the United Kingdom levy negligible taxes or none at all. Reconciliation of the differences is not likely before the mid-eighties.

As indicated in Chapter 3, courts in all member countries other than the Netherlands and the United Kingdom base their decisions in liability suits upon codified references to the issues, whereas British courts rule principally on the basis of judicial precedents and Dutch courts use both approaches. Also, whereas jurors hear actions in tort in the United Kingdom, judges alone make the decisions in such cases in the other countries. Because of those differences, the peril of loss through liability for damages differs within the Community. In general, where statutes closely define rights of recovery of persons injured through negligence of others and where jurors are not involved in civil actions, plaintiffs win only with much difficulty and receive lesser awards than they might have received in other countries. Inevitably, the differences in liability climates necessitate differences in insurers' claims reserves, in liability policies' limits of protections, premium rates, conditions and exclusions, and in insurers' underwriting practices. Unless the members take the unlikely step of adopting a common system of tort law, establishing a standard approach to the regulation of liability insurers will be difficult indeed.

Structural differences in the members' insurance markets constitute another obstruction to integration. The most significant is the impact of cartels. In Belgium, France, and Italy, domestic insurers have long shared the bulk of the business under agreements as to market shares, fields of specialization, premium rates, policy forms, and limits of insurers' liabilities. The German market was tightly cartelized in pricing by governmental order in 1964.[6] In the markets of the other members, cartels have exerted little or no influence.

Companies profiting from membership in cartels (in insurance or any other field) do not welcome the entry into their markets of aggressive and well-financed newcomers. Governments which relish the orderliness and stability in their markets produced by cartels do not appreciate challenges made by disruptive foreigners. Doing away with cartels in the foreseeable future, therefore, is unlikely, and the Community will not be able to regard its insurance market as fully integrated in that respect. However, the purposes behind insistence upon preservation of cartels are not necessarily inconsistent with the purpose underlying integration. Moreover, in some national markets participants in cartels and independent insurers have coexisted for decades. Conceivably, then, the commissioners eventually will agree to ground rules which will make feasible a mixture of insuring by cartel members and by independents.

Another marketing difference lies in the effect tariffs have on insurance prices. In most countries within the Community and elsewhere, associations of insurance companies long have published tariffs, i.e., specified charges to be incorporated into premium rates in recognition of designated hazards. Ostensibly, a government's purpose in tolerating the system is to protect policyholders against inability of insurers to pay claims due to ruinous price cutting. In fact, governments also are much interested in the flows of tax revenues which are proportionate to premium rates.

In some member countries, insurers customarily have charged their policyholders in full accordance with tariffs mainly because of governmental pressure. In others, insurers have virtually ignored such controls. For example, between the mid-sixties and late seventies, German insurers observed tariffs painstakingly, while companies in France and Italy undercut tariffs commonly, particularly for the benefit of large industrial policyholders.

The differences in attitudes toward the tariff system probably are not sufficiently divisive to halt integration permanently. Again, mixed markets—in this case, part tariff and part nontariff—have been commonplace. However, governments' need of premium tax revenue probably will broaden determination to force all insureds to pay tariff rates despite pleas of industrial and commercial companies that their casualty prevention practices, equipment, and personnel be recognized in the form of access to premium rates below tariffs.[7]

If a substantial degree of integration eventually develops, widened applicability of tariffs will not necessarily force all companies to pay tariff rates. If integration progresses sufficiently to enable companies to insure with carriers based in any of the member countries, they will be able to secure their protection in the member countries which sanction pricing apart from tariffs. Undoubtedly, however, some companies will be constrained by tactical considerations to secure all their insurance in their wholly tariff, domestic markets.

Significance of Britain's entry

Long before the United Kingdom became a member of the European Economic Community, many expected that its entry would hasten the move toward integration. Moreover, the charter members of the Commission assumed that British insurers' attitudes toward innovation, levels of insurers' earnings, comprehensive protection, speculation in risk bearing, international collaboration of insurers, and purposes of governmental regulation would have pronounced effects upon the operations of the market. Therefore, they regarded the years prior to Britain's entry as a period of marking time and deferred setting permanent ground rules.

Nevertheless, the Community's planners did not expect that the new market would be mainly a British institution, with French, German, Italian, and Scandinavian insurers handling small portions of the business. Instead, they believed that the functioning of a free-trade region of such size and diversity would so greatly strengthen the economies of all members that each country's insurers would transact the volume of domestic business they would have handled had the Community not been established and also that they would write substantial amounts of protection in other member countries.

After four years of British membership, none of those expectations had been realized. No perceptible acceleration in the speed of integration had occurred. Seemingly, the members' sectors of the market had not adopted the attitudes of British insurers. And the regions' insurers were not announcing new highs in profits.

However, perceptive viewers in Britain and on the continent felt that insurers throughout the Community were quietly contemplating the prospects of competing with the liberal and flexible British carriers in the huge arena to be known as the integrated market. Also, the viewers noted that the British presence had led to resumption of thought about and discussion of the pros and cons of "harmonization."

Implications of integration

An integrated market would benefit American corporations' affiliates which are administered largely by nationals and those closely controlled from the United States. The nationals who buy insurance tend to insure in their country's markets, employing the patterns of protection used by domestic companies. However, whether owned by nationals or foreigners, companies would have intriguing new opportunities to improve their insurance programs. They could buy—at prices made attractive by international competition—high limits of protection, multi-perils coverage, deductibles plans, and clauses fitted closely to needs. Also, they could take advantage of the most economical experience-rating plans and the maximum available credits for casualty prevention facilities.

American owner corporations which closely control their European affiliates likewise would have access to insurance choices which have not been readily available in the past. In addition to instructing its affiliates to adopt the insurance features listed above, an owner desiring coverage of its operations in several member countries under a blanket policy could buy the protection in whichever country it chose.

Undoubtedly, however, the views on insurance needs held by some of the nationals managing affiliates will not change with the evolution of the integrated market. Many such managers will ignore proposals to replace narrow covers with much broader ones. Others will refuse to spend the money necessary to buy the high limits which will be available. Some will be immobilized by stubbornness, while others will be driven by nationalism to employ only the plans of insurance long marketed by domestic insurers.

Latin American Common Markets

Operative in Latin America at the opening of the seventies were three common market organizations. The largest was the Latin American Free Trade Association; formed in 1960, it consisted of all Latin American companies other than Guyana. Also organized in 1960 was the Central American Common Market, with Costa Rica, El Salvador, Guatemala, Honduras, and Nicaragua as members.[8] Another subregional group is the Andean Common Market, established in 1969 by Bolivia, Chile, Columbia, Ecuador, and Peru. In 1976, Chile withdrew, and Venezuela changed its status from that of a particularly interested nonmember to a signer of the pact.

Underlying the formation of each was desire to improve economic conditions by promoting trade within the region, hastening industrial development, and increasing exports to nonmember countries. As in the European Economic Community, "harmonization" of economic policies was viewed by the planners as the route to the objectives. Unlike the European association, however, none of the Latin American groups planned to establish an integrated insurance market.

Details of most of the developments and frustrations constituting the early histories of the associations are beyond the scope of this chapter. Of particular significance, however, was a condition apparent in the early seventies. In none of the three had regionalism dissolved nationalistic restrictions upon the insuring of domestic affiliates of foreign owner corporations. Indeed, the Latin American Free Trade Association was so hampered by nationalism that it had accomplished little beyond holding meetings and publishing statistics.[9] Moreover, in the process of stimulating its members' economies, the Central American

Common Market had generated new nationalistic resentment of flows of premiums to insurers in the United States and Europe. (In the past, members' governments had been so little interested in insurance that they felt little unhappiness over exported premiums).

An early and important decision by the members of the Andean Common Market was to exclude foreign capital and management from numerous industries. Under the Cartegena Agreement's two-part plan, applicable to insurance and other fields of business, each member country bars additional foreign investment in insurance companies operating within its borders and, since 1974, moves toward ownership by nationals or government of at least 80 percent of each insurer's shares of stock. The members' expectation was that foreigners would control no domestic insurance companies by the close of the seventies.

The principal contributions of foreign owners to Latin American insurance markets have been competitive pressure and access to experience gained in other markets. With the lessening of these influences, the markets of the Andean countries may be less flexible than those of Europe or North America.

Governmental Controls

Nationalism and regionalism do not underlie all the controls imposed by law upon sellers and buyers of insurance. Regulatory statutes and administrative interpretations of statutes stem from a variety of attitudes and purposes. Consequently, such controls vary in form and in rigidity of enforcement. Also, in some countries they differ from one locality to another and, indeed, from one situation to the next.[10]

Mandatory Insuring

In almost all countries, companies are required to use one or more kinds of insurance. The most commonly required form provides medical and income benefits for employees disabled by job-caused accidents or illnesses. Social security programs of some countries also provide such benefits for persons disabled by causes unrelated to their occupations. Employers bear all or almost all of the costs under both systems. While they provide nonoccupational benefits via governmental agencies, in numerous countries they buy workmen's compensation protection from commercial insurers. However, they do not have the option available in the United States of meeting their workmen's compensation responsibilities by "self-insuring." Consequently, large companies which operate effective programs of on-the-job accident prevention cannot benefit fully from their superior loss records.

Compulsory use of auto insurance is very common. The countries of Europe and such other large-scale users of autos as Australia, Canada, Japan, and South Africa require auto owners to maintain auto liability insurance, and most European countries enforce no-fault laws, under which auto owners must buy insurance which will cover their medical costs and loss of income in event of accidents. Such laws are resented by companies which would prefer to absorb losses from auto accidents or to cover them under "world-wide" contracts rather than the prescribed policies issued by domestic insurers.

Much less common than the mandatory use of workmen's compensation insurance or auto insurance is compulsory insuring against fire.[11] Almost always the requirement is doubly intrusive inasmuch as it dictates also the amounts of insurance to be employed. Illustrative are local laws in Germany which require use of fire insurance in amounts equal to 100 percent of the values of buildings and a Brazilian law specifying that insurance apply to commercial and industrial buildings in amounts equal to at least 80 percent of values. Compliance with the latter law has been costly for property owners during Brazil's two decades of soaring real estate values.

Directors of risk control in American owner corporations resent not only the inclusion of coinsurance clauses in their policies but also the prohibition of systematic absorption of fire losses under deductibles or "self-insurance" plans.

Many laws requiring use of insurance specify the sources of the protection. Governments not only compel employers to pay for workmen's compensation benefits but also designate governmental bureaus as the insurers. In such exceptional countries as Brazil, Japan, and Venezuela, employers may buy workmen's compensation insurance from private companies or government agencies. Most compulsory auto insurance laws force auto owners to purchase their protection from domestic insurers, and Norway and Sweden license only a few companies to sell it.[12]

A government company, the Consorcio de Compensacio de Seguros, is Spain's monopolistic provider of insurance against loss from riot and civil commotion, from peacetime damage by military forces, and from wind, flood, volcanic activity, earthquake, and falling aircraft.[13] While the protection is not compulsory, each property owner who chooses to buy fire insurance must buy it also. A 15 percent surcharge on the fire premium finances the benefits. Because this unique plan pays only in the event of catastrophic loss from one of the indicated perils and because the Consorcio decides whether or not casualties were catastrophies, property owners who recover under the scheme are pleasantly surprised.[14]

Control of Policy Provisions

Inasmuch as all states in the United States interfere with insuring by requiring use of prescribed policy forms and clauses, management is not surprised to encounter similar controls in other countries. As in the most restrictive states, the regulatory bureaus of some countries require that insurers include in their policies only forms, clauses, or endorsements which have been approved by the bureaus. Consequently, policies issued in those countries consist of standard provisions only. A company facing risk requiring treatment under a nonstandard clause will obtain protection only if the regulatory authority grants special permission. Laws of numerous countries, including France, Germany, Italy, Japan, Mexico, and Spain, impose this restriction. However, evasion is commonplace, regulators conceding that total enforcement by their small staffs is impossible. In general, discrete inclusion of nonapproved clauses which are not detrimental to the policyholders is regarded by government as a practicable way of affording some flexibility.

Under a slightly less restrictive approach, laws require governmental approval of forms and clauses to be used in covering common situations of risk. By implication they permit use of nonapproved policy provisions in meeting unusual needs. A property damage policy applicable to a typical commercial building, for example, would consist entirely of standard provisions, while one applicable to a plant employing great quantities of a particularly volatile liquid could include—without prior approval—clauses tailored exclusively to the situation. Belgium employs this approach.

Another system requires use of statutory policy forms in the major fields of insurance. Argentinian law controls the wording of forms used in policies of fire, business interruption, ocean marine, and workmen's compensation insurance. Clauses attached to those statutory forms need not be approved, but they must not reduce the protection below that prescribed in the forms. Other users of this method include Brazil and Venezuela.

The most liberal countries require use of preapproved forms and clauses only in auto and workmen's compensation policies used in compliance with compulsory insurance laws; policies of other kinds can include whatever wording of forms and clauses the parties choose. However, regulatory authorities intercede if policyholders claim that they have been deceived or otherwise victimized in ways barred by codes of contracts. Less conflict between insureds and insurers occurs under such laws than might be expected because insurers avoid charges of misbehavior by voluntarily using forms and clauses which have become standard by usage, employing closely tailored clauses only in very unusual situations. Among the nations which have taken this liberal position are Australia, Denmark, the Netherlands, Norway, the United Kingdom, and Sweden.

By implication, such countries permit policies to be written which comply with other countries' requirements as to forms and clauses. Thus, a Michigan-based corporation which desires that policies applicable to its operations at home and abroad be as uniform as possible and which chooses to insure its Dutch affiliate in the Dutch market may ask the insurer to incorporate the forms and clauses required by Michigan law.

Control of Premiums

Where governments control premium rates, they do so in one or both of two ways. The less common method entails monitoring insurance prices and insurance companies' profits and compelling or pressuring insurers to reduce prices if, in the regulators' opinions, their profit margins are excessive. The Scandinavian governments and the government of Belgium continuously study insurers' operating results (and those of providers of all other kinds of goods and services) for indications that prices could be lowered without eliminating profits. Presumably, awareness of the surveillance prevents charging rates which might be difficult to justify, for governmental orders to reduce rates have been rare. Insofar as corporate users of insurance are concerned, moreover, the system offers little hope of government-ordered rate reductions. The regulatory bureaus feel that their mission is to protect individuals, not corporations.

The most used instrument of governmental rate control is the tariff. As a system of price fixing, it conceivably could accomplish its purpose of preventing reckless rate cutting without involvement of government. Almost always, however, government bureaus are involved in tariff operations. Some of them set premium rates, but in most countries associations of insurance companies perform that function.[15] In the many countries where tariffs apply to required auto and workmen's compensation insurance, bureaus judge whether tariffs proposed by the insurers' associations are equitable and enforce use of those tariffs they have approved.[16] Likewise, in some of the countries in which tariffs apply to noncompulsory insurances, laws require the regulators to enforce tariffs they have approved. Argentina, Belgium, Brazil, Japan, Mexico, Spain, and Venezuela are among them.[17]

The governments of France and Norway give or withhold approval of tariffs applicable to elective forms of insurance but do not have enforcement responsibilities. In still other countries, bureaus examine tariffs before they go into effect but do not have authority to bar them and do not enforce them. While this laissez-faire approach to private price fixing might seem likely to generate high premium rates, competition provided by insurers which have not agreed to observe the tariffs precludes setting rates which are unrealistically high. Denmark, Italy, the Netherlands, and the United Kingdom are in this category.[18]

Germany tightly controls premium rates through its rate cartels. A corollary of such control is rigidity in pricing. Negotiation of a special premium rate for an unusual situation of risk is almost impossible when the state is the price-fixing agency. In other countries—even those in which government bureaus enforce tariffs—discrete deviation from the tariffs occurs frequently.[19]

In general, the more rigidly tariffs are enforced, the more dissatisfied is corporate management. Where deviation from tariffs is rarely or never permitted, premium rates often are not closely attuned to hazards. Consequently, corporations which work systematically to prevent casualties are forced to subsidize corporations likely to experience more losses.

Control of Communications

In Japan and several other countries, statutes or administrative rulings require those in need of insurance to communicate with their prospective insurers only through the insurers' agents. Customarily, in those countries, each agent represents only one company. The effect of this combination of law and custom is to bar the prospective buyer from dealing through either a broker who would function as its agent in seeking out the insurer best suited to meet its needs or an "independent" agent representing numerous insurance companies and able, therefore, to weigh the qualifications of several insurers before recommending one.

Governments of several countries do not admit international brokers or agents of syndicates of American insurance companies even though they are not directed to bar them by law. They exclude such intermediaries by refusing to issue licenses to them. Regulators in

Italy, Spain, and Sweden are among those who use this technique. Through ties to domestic brokers, alien brokers and agents place some insurance in such countries, but domestic agents write the great bulk of the protection.

Venezuela excludes brokerage firms and agencies in which Venezuelans own less than 51 percent of the stock, thereby forcing foreign intermediaries into alliances with domestic firms much like those which have developed in the European countries indicated above.

Affiliates of American corporations which must insure via agents representing one domestic insurer each are likely to receive less information on developments in insurance than they would have obtained from brokers or agents who communicate with associates in many countries.

Overseeing loss settlements

In Brazil, settlements of large losses cannot be regarded by the parties as completed until the national goverment indicates its approval. Commonly, regulators enter negotiations at the request of policyholders who are dissatisfied with the offers of the insurers. On rare occasions they intercede without having been invited and issue unsought decisions.

Inflation

In addition to raising costs, inflation subjects corporate users of insurance to uncertainty as to whether their amounts of insurance will cover losses and meet coinsurance requirements.[20] Where amounts of insurance are indexed to increases in values of property or in court awards for damages, uncertainty is minimal, but the rising costs of insurance may be distressingly burdensome for some companies.

To cope with inflationary uncertainty in domestic or foreign operations, management must keep abreast of rising values. Ideally, the director of risk control monitors values in all countries in which his employer conducts operations and raises amounts of insurance in accordance with interests in values. If he does not control the insurance programs of foreign affiliates, he advises the affiliates' managers to make the adjustments.

Expanding of Inflation Problems through Governmental Acts

Some governments add to the ordinary difficulties experienced by insureds under rapid inflation. Those which demand inclusion of coinsurance requirements in standard property damage policies, almost always against the wishes of the insureds, force them into possibilities of coinsurance penalties. Among such governments are Argentina, Brazil, France, Mexico, and Spain.[21]

Brazil adds slightly to the cost of insurance by requiring that companies which are forced by inflation to increase their insurance do so not by raising limits of protection under existing policies but by purchasing supplementary policies. Applicable to a building, therefore, may be several policies, written successively over a brief period.

A particularly troublesome inflation problem is caused by the many governments which require that benefits under policies written in their markets be paid in their national currencies. Under this restriction, an affiliate of an American company which incurred fire damage to equipment which must be replaced from the United States might receive insurance proceeds far short of the amount needed for replacement or repair. If the amount of insurance had not been increased during the several months preceding the fire and if the domestic currency had depreciated more rapidly than the United States dollar during that period, the loss payment would convert to an inadequate number of dollars.

NOTES

1. All governments permit nonadmitted insurance companies to write ocean marine insurance applicable to shipments entering or leaving their countries.
2. Venezuela's law, for example, provides for fines amounting to twice the premiums that the violators would have paid had they insured domestically.
3. Ordinarily, a policy is in the language of the country in which it was written. Consequently, the director of risk control rarely can read policies written in affiliates' countries, and however carefully translators have converted policy wording into English, he cannot be certain that he has been provided with precisely the shades of meaning intended in the various markets.
4. The primary insurer, as lead underwriter, would negotiate the terms of the contract with the insured owner corporation.
5. Presumably, resident agents would represent insurers domiciled in most countries of the world.
6. Prior to the government's intercession, pricing practices were chaotic, according to a German observer, as insurers disregarded pricing agreements almost completely.
7. However restrictive such markets might be, the underwriters at Lloyd's probably will be permitted to continue to write insurance at rates below the tariffs. The need for their insuring capacity and their special services cause governments to treat them apart from orthodox insurers.
8. Honduras withdrew in 1970, following conflict with El Salvador, but subsequently

entered into separate trade agreements with each of the members other than El Salvador.

9. Formation of the Andean Common Market resulted partly from belief that the Latin American Free Trade Association was hopelessly immobilized by nationalism.

10. While internal differences are more common in the United States than elsewhere, division of power between national and state governments has this effect also in such countries as Australia, Germany, and Mexico.

11. Numerous countries require use of still other forms of insurance, applicable mainly to individuals. Examples are liability insurance for dog owners, hunters, accountants, and pharmacists, and accident insurance for student pilots. Also, Brazil requires companies to use several forms of insurance, including several types of liability coverage and marine insurance on shipments; and Argentina requires insuring (with Argentinian insurers) incoming shipments.

12. The United Kingdom's restriction represents a departure from the freedom otherwise afforded individuals and companies to buy their insurance wherever they please.

13. A deductible of 5 percent or a minimum of 1,000,000 pesetas applies to losses from all covered perils other than flood. The flood deductible is 20 percent or a minimum of 2,000,000 pesetas.

14. The plan fills a created lack in the Spanish market, for private insurance companies are barred from writing protection against the six extended coverage perils so widely covered by endorsement elsewhere. According to critics, the main consideration of the Consorcio in deciding whether floods, windstorms, or other occurrences have been catastrophes is whether or not its assets are at high levels.

15. Germany is an exception, with its government-controlled cartels as the writers of tariffs applicable to fire insurance.

16. The principal instrument of enforcement is the threat of punishment of insurers which deviate from tariffs. In Mexico, for example, an insurer which deviates without governmental approval may lose its license for three years.

17. Commonly, in such countries, tariffs are not applicable in all lines of insurance. In Brazil, Venezuela, and Japan, for example, they apply only in the fire, fire and auto, and fire, auto, and marine areas, respectively.

18. Italy, however, enforces life insurance tariffs strictly.

19. Spanish supervisory bureaus authorize deviation quite liberally. The Consorcio de Compensacio de Seguros, however, pays nothing to victims of loss for whom unauthorized deviations were arranged.

20. Because most property damage losses equal small fractions of the values of the property, only those loss victims which are grossly underinsured must absorb excesses of losses over insurance. Under policies which include coinsurance clauses, however, policyholders must bear portions of their losses if the amounts of their insurance are less than those required even though the protection greatly exceeds the losses.

21. In France the property owner has a choice of operating under the coinsurance clause or arranging for automatic increases in amount of insurance in accordance with an index of current values applicable to its type of building. Most policyholders choose the latter.

8

BARRIERS AND OPPORTUNITIES IN FOREIGN INSURANCE MARKETS

Governments are not the only producers of problems for American firms which use insurance abroad. Foreign insurance companies and their organizations for promulgating policy forms and premium rates impose rules and restrictions which are frustrating to American owner corporations. Described below are some of the annoyances they encounter in foreign insurance markets.

Of course, not all aspects of markets in other countries are unfavorable to policy holders. Attitudes and facilities in some markets enable American owners to insure their affiliates very effectively. Therefore this chapter also indicates some of those advantageous conditions.

Barriers

Disparagement of Comprehensive Risk Control

American directors of risk control have attitudes toward insurance usage which differ from those held by insurance companies in other countries. As practitioners in comprehensive risk control, they regard insuring and bearing losses out of pocket as secondary in importance to casualty prevention. They also believe that their main responsibility in the insuring process is to define needs and that the insurers' function is to meet those needs precisely. Managers of insurance companies in other countries, conversely, feel that casualty prevention and loss absorption are worth more as topics for academic discussion than as means of coping with risk. Most of them view efforts to prevent casualties as exercises in futility and systematic loss absorption as risk bearing by unrealistic dilettantes. Further, they believe that they are much better qualified than directors of risk control to ascertain insurance needs.

133

The attitude of insurers abroad toward casualty prevention is indicated by the small number of casualty prevention engineers the companies employ. Indeed, in most countries only American insurers and international brokerage firms employ qualified prevention specialists. France and all the countries of Latin America are among the nations with long established insurance industries which have trained few, if any, casualty prevention engineers. Countries in which the domestic insurers are young likewise are without such specialists.

The skepticism toward systematic loss absorption of insurers domiciled in most countries is not quite so pronounced as that directed toward casualty prevention; insurers in many countries include deductibles in policies and sometimes write excess protection above substantial exposures to out-of-pocket losses. Ordinarily, however, they do so reluctantly and agree to standard deductible amounts only. Moreover, in some countries—the Republic of the Philippines and Spain among them—domestic insurers refuse to write deductibles. And in Denmark, France, Germany, and Venezuela, insurers will include deductibles but discourage their use by granting negligible reductions in premium rates.

The presence in most markets of admitted American, British, and other foreign insurers enables some companies to insure with companies which are somewhat appreciative of the concept of comprehensive risk control.[1] However, many American owner corporations do not direct their foreign affiliates to insure exclusively with admitted foreigners. Some corporations have no choice; American or other foreign insurers sometimes cannot provide all the protection the affiliates need. Other corporations insure with domestic insurers if their premium rates are lower than those of the foreign insurers. Still others must defer to co-owners' preferences for insuring with carriers domiciled in their countries.

Thus, thousands of foreign affiliates of American corporations insure with domestic companies which regard insuring under highly standardized forms, clauses, and limits of protection as the only practicable form of risk control.

Inflexibility

The attribute of insurers abroad most frustrating to American owner corporations is inflexibility. In the forms of refusal to include nonstandard clauses in policies and refusal to charge appropriate nonstandard premium rates it is particularly irksome. The main barrier to adaptation to unusual conditions of risk is the tariff system of insurance pricing.[2] Under that system, insurers' associations—with governmental acquiescence—establish minimum premium rates for standard plans of insurance. Typically the associations do not welcome requests for use of nonstandard policy provisions and commensurate modifications of tariffs, partly because they cannot estimate the effects of the proposed changes upon loss ratios and party because they dislike change. Consequently, insurers which observe fire tariffs can write closely tailored deductibles plans only after overcoming stern opposition, if at all. Likewise, they rarely, if ever, can obtain permission to substitute 80 or 90 percent coinsurance requirements for the customary 100 percent clause. Even more irritating to American owner corporations are tariffs which ignore superior programs of casualty prevention and, in particular, fire prevention design and equipment which, in terms of American standards, would qualify premises for the designation "highly protected risk."

Among countries in which tariffs are enforced so rigidly that domestic insurers almost never ask for permission to use deviant clauses and premium rates are Argentina, Brazil, Belgium, and Spain.[3] Countries in which insurers petition occasionally but with little success are Italy, Japan, the Republic of the Philippines, the United Kingdom, and the Latin American countries other than Mexico and Venezuela. The latter two are notable for deviations from tariffs without the consent or knowledge of the associations. Unauthorized deviating occurs mainly where government exercises little control over the associations—by law or custom.

Where adherence to tariffs is not required by law, nontariff insurers operate in competition with the tariff companies. Ordinarily, nontariff markets consist entirely of admitted foreign insurers, and tariff markets of domestic companies. The nontariff markets provide flexibility in policy provisions and ratemaking like that practiced in the United States. As indicated above, however, some affiliates of American corporations do not use such flexibility.

In the many countries having little reinsurance capacity the restrictions imposed by foreign reinsurers upon domestic insurers cause inflexibility in pricing. For example, Belgian writers of machinery breakdown insurance cannot deviate from standard rates without the approval of their British, Swiss, French, or other foreign reinsurers.

Inflexibility as to policies' limits of protection also annoy American owner corporations. Mainly this is a problem encountered in the use of liability insurance, with domestic insurers in many countries denouncing the limits requested as absurdly high.[4] Some companies use the standard limits and hope that they will not be victimized by landmark awards of damages which greatly exceed the limits. Others instruct their affiliates to add layers of protection to the basic limits provided by the domestic insurers. Still others maintain world-wide excess policies to augment local limits.[5]

Indicative of basic per-occurrence bodily injury liability limits, in terms of United States dollars, are Argentina's and Brazil's limits of $500,000, Denmark's $330,000, Germany's $358,000, and the Republic of the Philippine's $100,000. Since American mangement is accustomed to limits of $10,000,000 or more in domestic operations and is fearful that awards for damages in other countries could soar far above usual levels, it regards use of excess contracts of insurance as necessary.

Indifferent Service

Inasmuch as insurers sell only service, indifference to the service function would seem to be a destructive attitude. Nevertheless it is an attitude common to many insurers in many countries, although insurers of no country are uniformly delinquent. Deficiencies in service are mainly in the forms of failure to move innovatively in writing and pricing protection and of delay in paying legitimate claims.

Domiciled in all countries are insurers which work diligently to devise the special policies and policy provisions some of their policyholders must have if they are to be protected fully and economically. Typically, they are handicapped in that effort by governmental and industry regulations. However, many of the failures of insurers to meet needs precisely cannot be blamed on regulators. Based in every country in which American owner corporations operate affiliates are insurers which are simply not disposed to devote the amounts of time and talent necessary to develop needed clauses or policies.

The underwriters at Lloyd's, London, are not among the insurers which are unable or unwilling to pursue innovation; they lead all other insurers in this form of service.

A form of poor service which is particularly costly to policyholders is delay in paying losses. Among countries in which insurers are chronically slow in responding to claims are France, Italy, and Spain. Some of the delays are due to procrastination, but others are intended to cause claimants lacking in perseverance to abandon their claims. A few delays relate to insurers' practice of paying only after the policyholders have attempted to collect damages from third parties who might have caused the casualties. Very often, incidentally, even when third parties finally have been found legally liable, their lack of money and insurance precludes their indemnifying their victims.

Barring Cancellation

The right of policyholders to cancel policies without seeking the agreement of their insurers is taken for granted in the United States. In some countries, however, the usual basis of cancellation is mutual assent of the parties; insureds are able to cancel unilaterally only after losses or if their insurers insist upon raising premium rates. Subject to such restriction are companies insured under ten-year fire policies in Belgium, Denmark, Germany, Italy, the Netherlands, and Spain.[6] In the Netherlands, moreover, companies insured under such policies must give notice three months in advance of intended dates of termination. However, some insurers include clauses permitting the insureds to cancel on the policies' anniversary dates.

Rejection of Useful Practices

Insurance companies in many countries refuse to employ practices regarded elsewhere as highly useful to policyholders and not unduly hazardous to insurers. The practices most commonly rejected are described below.

Refusal to write certain plans of insurance

Domestic insurers in some countries decline to insure affiliates of American owner corporations under plans which are not desired by domestic owners. Ordinarily, if American insurance companies are active in such countries, they are prepared to write the covers for domestic owners as well as for American corporations. However, American insurers sell very little of such protection to domestic companies because nationals assume that domestic insurers would be selling it if it were really useful. The number of users in almost any country, therefore, is very small, and the premium rates which the American insurers believe they must charge are very high. (Respecting the law of large numbers, they know that they cannot predict the amounts of loss which will occur and, therefore, place safety margins in their charges.)

Especially common abroad is insurer disinterest in protecting against loss through embezzlement. Managers of American corporations which insure against such theft feel that their companies' foreign affiliates should do so also. Nationals managing the affiliates, however, tend to regard fidelity coverage as unnecessary, having adopted domestic insurers' curious belief that employee dishonesty is an insignificant factor in cost of production. Often this difference in opinions is of no significance. With domestic insurers unwilling to write the amounts of embezzlement protection desired, the owner corporation is likely to agree with the affiliate to do without fidelity coverage. And if foreign insurers are willing and able to provide high limits but are forced by skimpy demand to charge very high rates, both owner and affiliate may decide against insuring.

Domestic insurers in Denmark and Spain write virtually no embezzlement insurance. (Spanish law prohibited writing this protection prior to the seventies.) In both countries the fidelity bonds markets consist of a few admitted foreign insurers. Venezuelan companies write very little protection against stealing of any kind, and even the foreign insurers cover embezzlement only as a favor to companies which have bought other forms of insurance from them.

Among countries in which employers can buy embezzlement protection from domestic carriers but cannot buy the forms of fidelity bonds which provide maximum protection are Belgium, Brazil, France, Mexico, and Venezuela. Domestic insurers in such countries, that is, do not write commercial blanket or blanket position bonds. A blanket bond protects the employer against loss through theft by any employee, thereby eliminating the guesswork which attends the use of a fidelity bond naming the few employees whose thefts would be covered. Because employees in all kinds of occupations can steal from their employers, the blanket approach is far more appropriate than name bonds everywhere.

Also unavailable through domestic insurers in most countries are property damage policies broad enough to cover the policyholder's property of all kinds, wherever located, against virtually all perils. Thus, domestic insurers in Argentina, Brazil, Denmark, France, Mexico, the Netherlands, Spain, and the United Kingdom write policies which provide adequate breadth of protection for perils covered but apply only to single locations. And thus, domestic carriers in Argentina, Brazil, Denmark, France, and the Republic of the Philippines, which are agreeable to covering virtually all the perils confronting their policyholders, insist upon insuring the various categories of property separately. In any of those countries, therefore, an affiliate which insures with a domestic company maintains separate policies applicable to its buildings, machinery and inventories of materials, and finished goods.

The packaging of several dissimilar perils—such as "all-risks" property damage, business interruption, theft by employees and outsiders, and legal liability in all its forms—is largely a practice of insurers in the United States, Canada, and the United Kingdom. Elsewhere, domestic insurers refuse to cover even two or three similar perils in single policies. Thus, insurers in Belgium, Brazil, Mexico, and the Netherlands not only are unwilling to couple crime and property damage protection but, like companies in France, Spain, Sweden, and Venezuela, refuse to write policies similar to the "Three-D," i.e., applicable to embezzlement and thievery of several other kinds. Norwegian insurers dislike the packaging approach in all its forms, refusing even to combine such areas of legal liability as products and premises.

Other plans which domestic insurers are not, ordinarily, prepared to write are: blanket machinery breakdown in Chile; business interruption in Mexico and Sweden; products liability in Italy; and reporting forms (providing flexible limits of protection) in Venezuela.

Refusal to adopt liberal approaches

Not all the domestic insurers of any given country take the same position, whether restrictive or liberal, on an issue, but one view or the other clearly predominates in each country. Outlined below are important restrictive practices employed in some markets despite abundant evidence that liberal alternatives are feasible.

In all countries, fire insurers pay for losses caused by negligence of their policyholders. In most countries, they employ the liberal approach, paying even when the insureds' gross negligence caused the fires. Among those which are restrictive in this regard are German and Italian insurers, who deny liability for fire losses resulting from policyholders' extreme and willful disregard for ordinary standards of care.[7]

Another issue in fire insurance is the effect a loss has upon the amount of protection given thereafter. Universally, a few decades ago, a policyholder's insurance was automatically reduced by the amount of its recovery. In the few countries where insurers continue to impose such reductions, policyholders which have effected recoveries tend to be underinsured—particularly if they have completed their replacement or repair of damaged property—unless they have replenished their protection by payment of additional premiums. Domestic insurers in Denmark and the Netherlands still write property damage insurance in this manner, refusing to state in their policies that limits of protection will not be reduced by amounts paid towards losses.

The most important difference in insurers' positions in writing property damage insurance is in the valuation of the insurer's liability in event of loss. Under the liberal approach, the insurer bears the full cost of repair or replacement of damaged buildings, equipment, or inventories. Under the restrictive plan, the insurer pays the actual cash value of the loss, i.e., the cost of repair or replacement minus depreciation which had occurred prior to the fire or other casualty.[8] Insurers in numerous countries have written both actual cash value and replacement cost contracts since the fifties or sixties, but domestic insurers in some markets (among them Chile, Japan, and Spain) still insure only on the basis of actual cash value. Mexican insurers are willing to write replacement cost contracts but do so only for premium rates 150 percent of actual cash value rates.[9]

Several contrasts have developed in liability insurance. For example, the liberal position holds the insurer liable for injuries and damage arising out of "occurrences" whereas the restrictive approach requires it to pay for consequences of "accidents." Under a policy written on the "accident" basis, it is liable only if the insured inflicted injury or damage by an act, or a failure to act, at an identifiable point in time. Causing an illness gradually by exposing the victim to poisonous gases over several months does not qualify as an "accident"; it is an injurious "occurrence." Domestic insurers in Australia and Chile are among those which have not converted to writing liability insurance on the "occurrence" basis.

Italian and Mexican insurers favor the restrictive approach in bearing policyholders' costs of defense against suits for damages. The limits on their liabilities specified in their policies apply to defense costs as well as to awards or out-of-court settlements. Under the liberal arrangement, insurers bear defense costs without limit; their policies' stated limits apply only to settlements or awards.

Another example of the illiberal approach to liability insurance: in a few countries policies are written on the basis of indemnity. Thus, Australian and Italian insurers pay only after their policyholders have paid out of pocket to claimants. Under this system, conceivably, an insurer need pay nothing if its policyholder was unable to pay the damages awarded his victim. In practice, however, some insurers regard this system as more theoretical than real, and they routinely observe the liberal approach by paying the claimant on behalf of the policyholder.

In providing business interruption insurance, the most notable difference in attitude concerns eligibility for benefits. Policies issued by Belgian and French insurers bar payment of benefits to insureds which are not working to restore their damaged premises to full usage. The insurer pays nothing to a policyholder which is not rebuilding its plant even though the damage prevents the plant from generating income sufficient to cover fixed costs and produce net earnings.

In the other countries considered here domestic writers of business interruption insurance pay even to policyholders which announce after their fires or other casualties that they do not intend to rebuild: they pay amounts equal to the fixed costs and net profits the policyholders would have covered with revenues they would have produced during the period of time they would have spent working with due diligence and dispatch to make repairs and replacements.

Markets' Deficiencies

Many companies cannot insure to the satisfaction of their American owner corporations because the domestic markets have inadequate facilities. The deficiencies are attributable to inadequate flows of revenues caused either by the presence of more domestic insurers, brokers, and adjusters than are needed to handle the small amounts of business or by governmental price control. Insurers writing small volumes of premiums cannot afford highly effective employees and cannot spend much on training, research, and experimentation. Similarly, skimpy commissions bar domestic brokers from employing talented persons, and scarcity of fees for adjusting losses retards expansion in that field. If domestic manufacturers and merchants continue to use only a few kinds of insurance and to buy low limits of protection, these financial constraints will persist indefinitely in many countries.[10]

Lack of casualty prevention engineering

In most countries, the indifference of top management toward casualty prevention and the inadequate financial resources of domestic insurers and brokers preclude spending much money on casualty prevention. In all countries the large domestic insurers perform fire prevention inspections, but in all except Canada and the United States the quality of that service is consistently low. Even in Japan and the highly industrialized countries of Europe, companies do not expect their domestic insurers to conduct frequent and intensive inspections.

In many markets the only insurers which spend substantially on prevention are outposts of American companies, and the only brokers doing so are the large international firms and some of their local correspondents. In Japan, for example, American insurers and brokers maintain the country's largest resident staffs of prevention engineers. Because those specialists work mainly with the few affiliates of American corporations, the great bulk of the country's industrial and mercantile companies obtain little or no help in prevention from insurers or brokers.

Where domestic prevention engineers are available, American owner corporations regard them as less experienced than those employed by insurers or brokers based in the United States. Consequently, an American owner corporation having an affiliate in the Netherlands, for example, demands that its broker send fire prevention engineers to make periodic inspections of the affiliate's plant despite the fact that the broker's Dutch correspondent employs fire prevention specialists who are readily available.

Shortage of independent adjusters

In many countries companies which find themselves in need of help of independent adjusters to effect recoveries under their policies learn that expert adjusters are scarce. Japan, Norway, and Spain are virtually without them. Italy has few adjusters who have extensive experience in negotiating recoveries of business interruption losses. In Argentina and Mexico, very few persons are experienced in assisting affiliates of foreign companies to recover from insurers. Adjusters in Brazil are government employees and are so scarce that policyholders often must wait for many months for recovery. (Mexican adjusters, however, are regarded as highly competent.)

Minimal influence of foreign insurers

The presence in an insurance market of large, progressive foreign insurers is desirable not only for their policyholders but also for companies insuring with domestic carriers. The local insurers are forced to meet policyholders' needs lest they lose customers to vigorous foreign competitors. The underwriters at Lloyd's, London, for example, have for centuries forced competitors in many countries to improve their protection or reduce their premium rates. Markets lacking foreign insurers, therefore, annoy American owner corporations.[11]

The number of foreign insurers and the influence they exert on their markets vary greatly from country to country. Active in France are over 200 foreign insurers, in Belgium, 75, and in Italy, 50. The Mexican market, conversely, has only one foreign-controlled insurer—an association insuring in behalf of its American corporate members. Presumably, in view of its determination that all insurers be owned completely by Mexican nationals, the government will evict the association or require that it be dominated by domestic members. In Denmark, Lloyd's brokers constitute the only foreign presence. (Under contracts with foreign insurers, however, some Danish insurance agents place insurance with them.) In Venezuela, nationals must own at least 51 percent of the common stock of every company writing insurance. That requirement has not eliminated foreign influence upon policies and premiums but is reducing it. Finally, although numerous foreign insurers do business in the markets of Norway and Sweden, a general preference for contracting with Scandinavian insurers restricts their influence.

Defective reinsurance facilities

Insurance markets of many countries have several defects: complete, or almost complete, dependence upon foreign reinsurers; laws requiring insurers to obtain their reinsurance from domestic reinsurance companies or from the government's reinsurance bureau; presence of very few reinsurance companies.

From the standpoint of the foreign affiliate of an American owner corporation, the absence of domestic reinsurers in the insurance market in its country is not necessarily an unfortunate situation; if domestic reinsurers were in the market, they might be unsatisfactory. However, if the market included high-quality domestic reinsurers as well as foreigners, it would benefit from price competition between the domestic and foreign reinsurers.

No reinsurers are domiciled in Belgium or Norway. The markets of Mexico, the Netherlands, and Spain include only a few small reinsurers each.

Laws barring domestic insurance companies from reinsuring with foreign companies deprive domestic insurers of the benefits of competition. Exclusion of the dozen huge European reinsurers from a market may encourage the shielded domestic reinsurance companies to operate as a cartel. If not, it may induce the monopolistic government reinsurer to base premium rates on whatever considerations it pleases and to force primary insurers to include whatever policy provisions it regards as desirable.

As indicated in Chapter 7, Japanese law requires primary insurers to secure their reinsurance—with the exception of that applicable to policies of earthquake insurance—from domestic reinsurance companies. Mexico has moved toward reserving reinsurance business for Mexican companies by demanding that at least 50 percent of reinsurance applicable to fire risks be written by domestic companies. Governmental agencies operate reinsurance monopolies in Argentina, Brazil, and Chile, while France requires primary insurers to secure 40 percent of their reinsurance from a governmental insurer.

Policyholders whose insurers reinsure in markets which consist of only a few reinsurers are adversely affected. If the reinsurers choose to charge high rates, the primary insurers must charge correspondingly high premiums unless they are able to reinsure abroad. Moreover, if the reinsurers are unwilling to sanction experimentation with new plans of insurance or modifications of standard policies, they forbid the primary insurers to make the changes. Among such markets are those of Germany and Italy. In Germany, the attitudes of one very large reinsurer and two slightly smaller ones affect the protection and premiums of virtually all corporate users of insurance. (Indicative of the financial capacity of the largest of the three is the fact that a small part of its foreign business is the reinsuring of almost the entire Greek primary market.) Italian insurers are free, under law, to reinsure with whichever domestic or foreign reinsurers they please. However, so many are restricted, in their ceding of insurance, by ties to banks and other companies associated with three large reinsurers that those reinsurers constitute, in essence, the market. Consequently, the three have an impact upon the charges and practices of primary insurers in Italy similar to that of the German trio upon carriers in their country.

Excluding or restricting foreign brokers

Because they are not under contract to represent specified insurance companies, ordinarily brokers offer, as their primary form of service, the ability to link their clients to whichever insurers are best fitted to meet the clients' needs. Another important service of international brokers, as indicated above, is providing guidance based upon their expanding stores of information on perils, laws, and behavior of regulators.

Laws of many countries bar foreign brokers. Some are even more restrictive, hampering communication between foreign brokers and their domestic correspondent brokers by forbidding employees of the former from entering the latters' countries for business purposes. Under that restriction, American brokers' executives, engineers, and underwriters can enter correspondents' countries only on the pretext of seeking relaxation or cultural development.

In some countries, insurance brokerage is illegal by implication. By not recognizing the concept of brokerage, legislators have implied that it is not an authorized vehicle of business. Foreign brokers are not thereby excluded completely from such markets, for they can work through insurance agents in some of the countries and communicate with clients in others by telephone and mail from neighboring countries. Clearly, however, foreign brokers' ability to serve under such conditions is limited. More of their time and money must be spent in fact-finding and negotiation of insurance contracts than in more favorable situations. Denmark, Italy, Japan, Mexico, and Sweden prohibit brokerage in this way. With neither brokers nor independent agents in Denmark and very few of either in the Italian market, American and other foreign brokers cannot work with clients in those countries through intermediaries.[12] Therefore, they communicate with their Danish clients from the Netherlands and with Italian companies from Austria or France.

Foreign brokers are able to transact business in Japan by obtaining licenses as agents of Japanese or admitted foreign insurance companies. Foreign brokers which have clients in Sweden associate with agents, each representing one domestic insurer. Through affiliation with agents representing the country's strongest and most helpful insurers, a foreign broker is in a position to choose the insurer best suited to protect the client.

While Mexican law does not recognize insurance brokerage, the government tolerates the presence of a half-dozen domestic brokerage firms. All write large volumes of business, and all are affiliated with American brokers or are familiar with their modes of operation. Governmental awareness that the domestic insurance companies need the guidance of sophisticated brokers underlies this tolerance.

Spanish law permits only Spanish individuals (not corporations) to engage in insurance brokerage. In order to do business in Spain, the foreign brokerage firm must work with an individual Spanish national. Unfortunately for the firm, the individual may lack experience and the means of employing informed assistants and, consequently, may need costly coaching by the firm.

Market Institutions

Exclusive systems of marketing

In insurance markets rated "superior" by purchasers, insurers use four marketing methods. The insurers known as "direct writers" employ salaried agents; others use agents representing them only, although earning commissions rather than salaries; some deal with agents who are independent, in that each can place business with any of several insurers; and some use brokers. Where all four approaches are in use, a company in need of insurance has access to the maximum range of premiums and of insurers' services.

In none of the countries considered here are all four methods in use. Indeed, one method—brokerage—is used to the virtual exclusion of the others in Argentina, Belgium, Brazil, France, and the United Kingdom.

Chile, Denmark, Mexico, the Netherlands, Norway, and Spain are dual-systems markets, with most insurers writing through agents representing them exclusively. The less used method in Denmark and the Netherlands is direct writing; in the others, brokerage. Insurers in Italy, Japan, the Republic of the Philippines, and Sweden also use two systems. Most Italian and Swedish companies are direct writers, but some work with agents of the single-principal variety—mainly when such agents represent international brokers. Philippine insurers usually write through single-principal agents but do some business with independent agents. In Japan, domestic insurers write mostly through single-principal agents, whereas foreign insurers and a few domestic carriers use employee agents.

Employed in Australia, Germany, and Venezuela are three of the methods. Brokerage and direct writing are common practice in all three. In addition, independent agents are used in Australia and Germany, and single-principal agents in Venezuela.

Minimal competition among insurers

The cartel, an old institution in European business, minimizes policyholders' choices of insurers, policy provisions, and premium rates, and in the long run it tends to deter insurers from striving to improve service. In the full meaning of the word (i.e., an association formed to restrict competition), all tariff associations are cartels and therefore are important factors in pricing in virtually all insurance markets. Particularly detrimental to price competition are the rate-making cartels in Brazil, Chile, and the Netherlands; not only do they rarely permit deviations, they require even admitted foreign insurers to observe the tariffs.[13]

Narrowly defined, the cartel's purpose is to limit competition by assigning business territories to members. Italy's Concordat performs that function and, to some extent, also specifies the plans of protection to be written by particular member companies. Further, as a tariff association it polices members' pricing and policy-writing practices.

Licensing only a few insurers to write insurance of a particular kind clearly limits competition and has the same adverse effects upon insureds as the operation of cartels. Among countries considered here, such licensing applies mainly to workmen's compensation insurance. Among governments designating the small numbers of insurers which can write this compulsory form of insurance are those of Australia, Belgium, Denmark, and Italy. The Italian government authorizes only two government-operated insurers to provide the protection.

The French government exercises an unusual form of market restriction, permitting only specially licensed brokers in major port cities to place ocean marine insurance. In the smaller ports, it permits all marine brokers to arrange such protection.

Controlled insurance companies

In the many countries in which insurance companies are owned by banks or by owners of banks, the companies tend to work less diligently than independent insurers to meet policyholders' needs. Assured of large volumes of business with the banks' debtors, they need not provide outstanding service in order to cope with competitors. Among countries in which this condition has led to inadequate but costly programs of insurance are Brazil, Italy, and Spain. In those three countries, banks dominate some of the largest domestic insurers.

A similar market defect exists in Japan, where five fleets of large companies—including insurers—are owned by dynastic families. American observers feel that the insurance companies in such fleets are under much less competitive pressure than independent insurers inasmuch as the other companies in their fleets and many outsiders under obligation to fleet members must insure with them.

Policy warranties

In the United States, as elsewhere, courts permit insurers to avoid liability for losses on ground of insureds' breaches of warranties in their policies. However, American owner corporations have experienced unpleasant surprises abroad in the form of courts' findings of breaches of warranties they had not realized were in their affiliates' policies.

In Brazil, for example, oral descriptions by an applicant for insurance of fire fighting apparatus in its building may be held to be a warranty that the equipment will be on the premises, unchanged in condition, throughout the policy period. If the equipment was not available or had deteriorated at the time of a fire, the insurer probably would avoid liability on ground of breach of warranty. In most jurisdictions in the United States, courts regard such descriptions as representations and permit insurers to avoid liability only on evidence that inaccuracies therein lured the insurers into harmful decisions as to whether to write the protection or as to premium rates.

Under French and Italian law, policyholders' descriptions in their fire policies of features of construction and of uses of their buildings are warranties. Consequently, breach of such a warranty by describing inaccurately would bar the policyholder from recovery. Most courts in the United States would not treat such statements as warranties unless they were prefaced by such unequivocal phrases as "the insured warrants."

Crudity in pricing

A complaint of American directors of risk control about tariffs in most countries is that they do not closely reflect the hazards in many situations of risk. For example, fire insurance premium rates in Australia do not relate closely to policyholders' standards of housekeeping despite the fact that housekeeping clearly bears heavily upon probabilities of fire.[14] Such indifference to the degree of hazards results in careful policyholders' subsidizing slovenly policyholders.

Commonly, too, tariffs force insurers to give inadequate rate reductions for installation of automatic sprinklers. In Brazil and Venezuela, in particular, companies which vastly improve their ability to fight fires in that manner earn token reductions in fire premium rates. Whereas sprinkler systems in the United States and a few other countries earn reductions of as much as 80 percent, Brazilian and Venezuelan property owners receive credits of 10 percent or slightly more. In many countries, the credits cluster around the 45 percent level and are inequitably low.

Conditions other than rigidity of tariffs underlie some of the crudity in insurance pricing. Insurers in the Philippines price their protection against losses from earthquake, typhoon, and volcanic eruption crudely because they feel they have no alternative. They reason that they cannot closely relate policyholders' premium rates to the locations of their buildings because they believe that the surges of energy in earthquakes and typhoons follow predictable routes, and, therefore, premium rates applicable to buildings in hazardous areas would have to be unbearably high.

Fire insurers in other countries which are particularly susceptible to earthquake either exclude fire damage caused by earthquakes or relate premium rates to the geographical zones in which the property is located. While they do not establish the zones arbitrarily, they are making mere gestures toward scientific pricing; forecasting where earthquake damage will occur and the extent of damage it will wreak is not yet an exact science.

Opportunities

In using foreign insurance markets, American owner corporations face many more barriers than opportunities. Therefore, they cannot afford to overlook any of the opportunities.

Liberal Practices

Liberality in insurers is evidenced chiefly by willingness to consider deviating from standard practices. It occurs on two levels: the insurers in some markets are more liberal, collectively, than those in other markets; in every market, some insurers are more liberal than their competitors. The markets named below are outstanding because of the liberal positions taken by their domestic insurers. As indicated, they are selectively liberal; a market which is liberal in one regard may be illiberal in another.

Pricing

The Belgian ocean marine insurance market is liberal in its pricing. Instead of following the lead of the British market, as do insurers in most other countries, the Belgians tend to charge rates which are surprisingly low. Some of their rates are speculative, based upon intuitive views of marine hazards. Most, however, rest upon analyses of hazards which produce findings different from those of insurers in other markets.

Venezuelan providers of business interruption insurance also stand apart in their willingness to charge premium rates substantially lower than those charged in other countries. Whereas business interruption rates in most countries amount to approximately 85 percent of fire insurance rates, Venezuelan rates ordinarily equal about 20 percent. The Venezuelan insurers have rejected the rationale behind business interruption rating in other markets and price on the basis of findings regarding conditions in their country.

In most countries suffering from chronic, substantial inflation, insurers favor writing policies for terms of one year or less so that they can raise premium rates frequently. Argentinian property damage insurers differ, writing fire policies at fixed rates for three- and five-year periods and granting sizable discounts for insuring for such periods.

As indicated above, Mexican insurers demonstrate liberality in their unauthorized charging of premium rates below those established by their tariff associations. When they believe that the tariffs do not provide superior risks with adequate rate credits and are certain that the associations would not correct the inequities, they discreetly award discounts.

Writing policy provisions

In the opinion of American management, the ultimate in liberal insuring would be the issuance of liability policies specifying no limits of protection. With courts in the United States awarding damages in ever larger amounts, management cannot be certain that the ceiling on its liability insurance—whatever its height—is high enough. French insurers offer liability protection which approaches the ultimate inasmuch as their policies do not include per-occurrence or per-accident limits on bodily injury liability. (They specify per-occurrence limits on property damage liability, however.) The policies are not really without limits, for they include an aggregate annual limit of F10,000,000. Nevertheless, in France that limit is so high in comparison with damages awarded by the courts that very few companies will have annual aggregate losses approaching it. Single losses of that magnitude are almost inconceivable. Not all French insurers offer this plan, however. Those which do place the French market on an exclusive level of liberality.

Another liberal practice is the providing of payment of benefits in United States dollars rather than national currencies. In no countries are domestic insurers enthusiastic about this practice and in most they do not even consider it. Japanese insurers probably write more dollar policies (in proportion to their total writings) than insurers of any other country. Their liberality, in that regard, is not confined to the dollar; they are more or less agreeable to paying claims in any currency, provided that the insureds pay premiums in the same currency.

Other countries in which insurers sometimes insure in dollar terms and thereby set their markets apart from the majority are Denmark, France, Germany, the Netherlands, Norway, Spain, and Sweden. German, Dutch, Norwegian, and Swedish insurers write dollar policies in all areas of insurance. Those in Denmark, France, and Spain are less liberal, insuring for dollar amounts only in the ocean marine area.

English language policies

Upon request, domestic insurers of a few countries write policies in English. This practice entails more than instructing linguists to convert policies' words into English. Insurance terminology differs from market to market, and only persons thoroughly familiar with the differences can translate words and phrases into exact equivalents in other languages. Sometimes, moreover, perfect translation is impossible; insurance concepts recognized in one market may not have exact counterparts in another. Because of these difficulties and because faulty translation leads to dispute and resentment, insurers in most countries refuse to write insurance in foreign languages. Consequently, most foreign affiliates of American owner corporations are insured under policies written in the languages of their countries, and the corporations' managers are chronically fearful that translators have failed to provide English versions which convey the exact shades of meaning intended by those who wrote the policies.

Domestic Belgian and Norwegian insurers are more willing than those of the other countries considered here to write policies in any of several foreign languages. Italian insurers are somewhat liberal in this regard, agreeable to writing in English but rarely in other languages.

Useful Market Facilities

Insurance markets vary widely in mental and financial resources. Indicated below are exceptional facilities afforded by some markets.

Superior service

Domiciled in several of the markets examined here are insurers with international reputations for superior management. Led by persons of outstanding ability and integrity, they are admired for the skills and deportment of their employees. They loom above domestic and foreign competitors in knowledge of insurance, awareness of and ability to evaluate hazards, and adaptability. Their premium rates are not necessarily the lowest in their markets, but they have earned respect for the zeal with which they strive to price equitably. While they are not necessarily the largest insurers in their countries, they are so profitable and so financially conservative that no one ever wonders if they may have difficulty in meeting claims. And while they do not pay claims without having established their validity, they pay legitimate claims promptly and in full. Based in Brazil, Italy, Germany, Sweden, and the United Kindom are insurers ranking among the best managed in the world.[15] Some operate only in their domestic markets; some have subsidiaries in numerous countries.

Competent brokers may be as valuable to owner corporations as sound insurers. Brokers with exceptional skills in risk analysis and exceptional knowledge of insurance markets can enable corporations to surmount the difficulties imposed by distance and language in overseeing the insuring of foreign affiliates.

In none of the markets in which brokerage is lawful are the practitioners uniformly competent. Obviously, the 4,000 brokers active in Paris and its suburbs cannot be equally experienced in meeting the insurance needs of corporations. Obviously, too, one broker of the half-dozen in another market can be outstanding for his intelligence and experience. In almost any market, however, at least a few brokers are well equipped to meet the needs of foreign owners' affiliates. The international departments of the major American brokerage firms have expertly staffed outposts in many overseas markets and have active relationships with able domestic brokers in most of the others. In some markets, moreover, unaffiliated domestic brokers are highly informed and conscientious. In each of the following countries, for example, several unaffiliated brokers add greatly to the worth of the markets: Argentina, Australia, Belgium, France, Germany, Mexico, the Netherlands, Norway, the United Kingdom.

Ample capacity

From the standpoint of the corporate user of insurance, an insurance market has adequate capacity if (a) its primary insurers can retain substantial portions of the risks they write and can readily reinsure the remainder, or (b) the primary insurers can readily obtain all the reinsurance they need without paying excessive reinsurance rates or having to include restrictive provisions in their policies.[16]

Markets which are notable for their ability to meet without strain all domestic need of insurance and reinsurance include those in France, Germany, Italy, the Netherlands, the United Kingdom, and Venezuela. Much of the great capacity of the Netherlands is generated by the Amsterdam-Rotterdam Bourse, a unique marketplace to which brokers bring risks for insuring by corporate insurers. Numerous primary insurers in Britain, the Netherlands, and Italy have very large capacities. Furthermore, all primary insurers in those countries have access to huge domestic reinsurance capacities and can reinsure as they please in foreign markets. Some markets afford ample capacity because their primary insurers are free to reinsure abroad and can do so at moderate costs. Among such markets are those of the Philippines and Spain.

Nontariff lines

Markets in which insurers price all policies in accordance with tariffs are rarities. In almost all countries, admitted foreign insurers write protection mainly on the nontariff basis, and domestic insurers write a few forms of insurance which are not included in the tariff structures. In theory, pricing in the nontariff lines is competitive. In fact, almost all the insurers closely follow the lead of dominant carriers in setting their rates.

The most common nontariff field is liability insurance. Among markets in which insurers can sell liability protection without reference to tariffs are those of Argentina, Belgium, Chile, Denmark, France, Germany, Italy, Japan, Mexico, the Netherlands, the Republic of the Philippines, and Spain.[17]

Other nontariff lines are boiler and machinery insurance in France, inland marine in Norway, Spain, and the United Kingdom, and ocean marine in Belgium, the Netherlands, and the United Kingdom.

Special Protection

Insurance markets differ greatly in details of plans of protection. Among those deserving recognition because their insurers offer useful features not available in most markets are those indicated below.

Protection against underinsuring

With malignant inflation an almost universal plague, great numbers of companies in most parts of the world fail to maintain amounts of property damage insurance sufficient to cover their losses or to comply with their coinsurance requirements. In some countries, however, property owners do not fear that property damage losses will greatly exceed the amounts of their insurance or that they will recover only partially in consequence of failure to maintain ratios of insurance to value prescribed in coinsurance clauses. Behind such assurance in the Netherlands is a statute requiring insurers to calculate the values of the buildings they cover every two and one-half years. If the policyholder raises the amount of insurance on its buildings in accordance with those valuations, it is immune to the penalties of insuring inadequately.

Swedish law requires no such appraisals, but the country's largest property insurer encourages its policyholders to examine their insurance needs systematically by offering to perform annual appraisals at negligible charges. The key to its ability to charge very little for a form of service which ordinarily is quite costly is its use of a method enabling the appraiser to establish the value of a building in no more than twenty minutes.

The most common method for coping with inflationary rises in property values is indexing. It entails the insurer's raising the policyholder's amounts of insurance—periodically and automatically—as indices reveal increases in values of buildings and equipment. Governments supply the indices used in some systems, insurers' associations in others. Because 100 percent coinsurance requirements apply in the countries using this approach, the effect is maintenance of insurance equal to the full value of the property throughout the policy term. To qualify for the adjustability, the policyholder initially permits its insurer to perform detailed appraisals of its property and bears the costs thereof. Managers who are aware of the huge coinsurance penalties or of the large gaps between amounts of loss and amounts of insurance their companies otherwise might encounter do not resent bearing the appraisal charges and the automatic increases in premiums which are a part of indexing. Countries in which most property insurers practice indexing are Argentina, Belgium, Denmark, France, Germany, Italy, and Norway.[18]

Italy's insurers also enable policyholders to guard against underinsuring in the use of business interruption insurance. They offer an endorsement providing for increase of the policy's stated limit of protection by as much as 30 percent if the need occurs. The plan does not eliminate the possibility of underinsurance, but it provides a margin of safety which ordinarily is adequate.

Broad covers

Domestic insurers in the markets of most countries write property damage policies applicable to groups of perils. Ordinarily, all the insurers in any market offer the same package. Illustrative are the combinations the domestic insurers of Argentina, Australia, France, Germany, Mexico, Norway, the United Kingdom, and Venezuela write for their commercial and industrial policyholders. They include the basic perils, fire and lightning, and an approximate dozen of the other standard perils which insurers in the United States tie to those two. In other markets, insurers provide breadth of property damage protection not by specifying numerous perils but by combining a few perils which insurers in most countries insist upon covering under separate contracts. Thus, domestic insurers in Belgium, Brazil, Chile, Italy, the Netherlands, Spain, and Sweden write policies covering both fire and steam boiler explosion.

Exemplifying breadth of liability protection is the Comprehensive General Liability insurance policy offered in the United States. It is approximated, however, by broad liability policies offered by domestic insurers in Argentina, France, and Germany. Indeed, in terms of the modest dimensions of the liability peril in those countries, the policies are almost as comprehensive as the Comprehensive General Liability policy. Almost as broad is liability protection provided by domestic insurers in Brazil and the United Kingdom.

The world's broadest plan of theft insurance is the Comprehensive Dishonesty, Disappearance and Destruction policy, enabling a company in the United States to insure under a single policy against employee theft and four other kinds of stealing. The only important form of theft excluded is shoplifting. Among insurers outside the United States which offer approximations of the "Three-D" policy are domestic carriers in Italy and admitted American insurers in Australia and the Republic of the Philippines. In other markets, corporations can secure the breadth of protection available under the "Three-D" by buying separate covers. Among markets offering such assortments of theft policies are those of Argentina, Germany, Japan, the Netherlands, and Norway.

Unusual covers

Insurers in some markets are more venturesome than most American companies, writing protection routinely against risks regarded in the United States as uninsurable or insurable only under unusual circumstances. Thus, a German company and an Italian company, both operated by the national governments, insure domestic companies against losses in foreign investments through expropriation or other harmful governmental acts. Likewise, British insurers—one owned by the government, one by investors—write export credit insurance, shielding exporters against loss through customers' defaults following political convulsions or collapse of national economies. Another example is that of the numerous German insurers who write machinery installation insurance, indemnifying for damage to machinery during installation or use. Written on the all-risks basis, it provides exceptionally broad protection, covering damage caused not only by accidents of all kinds but also by errors in design and acts of vandals and saboteurs.

In countries which are especially exposed to natural disasters, domestic insurers offer some protection. Insurers in Chile, Japan, Mexico, and Spain provide earthquake insurance and, in Mexico, protection against volcanic eruption as well. While they cannot write the policy limits needed by many of their policyholders, they provide insurance applicable to perils which could bring loss to high percentages of their insureds simultaneously.[19]

Among the few countries in which domestic insurers write flood insurance are Argentina, Chile, France, Japan, and Spain. In each of those markets, with the exception of Spain where the government-operated consortium described in Chapter 7 is the sole provider of the protection, the writers of flood insurance are private companies. They recognize the uninsurability of the flood peril, writing it only under governmental pressure or in accommodation of insureds which also buy kinds of insurance which they can provide profitably. An example of the universal awareness of the dangers in writing flood insurance is the Japanese government's permitting insurers to charge premium rates which are much higher than the prices of other forms of property insurance.

NOTES

1. The United States-based insurers which do business as admitted companies in many countries are American Foreign Insurance Association, American International Underwriters, and Insurance Company of North America. FM Insurance Company, Limited, is increasingly active in European markets, and Aetna Life and Casualty, Chubb and Sons, and Kemper Insurance are each in several markets. Lloyd's, London, is represented by brokers in many markets. Some of the British, Swiss, and Italian insurers admitted to numerous markets are, like the American companies above, attuned to the comprehensive risk control concept.

2. Fire insurance tariffs are operative in almost all the countries of the world. Tariffs are common also in business interruption insurance and marine insurance.

3. By law, all insurers in Spain observe the tariffs.

4. Almost never do insurers refuse to issue the amounts of property damage insurance desired by owner corporations inasmuch as governments of many countries require building owners to maintain the 100 percent ratio of insurance to value in order to obtain as much as possible in premium taxes.

5. Excess levels of liability insurance are not available in some markets, Denmark among them. Domestic insurers and the governments in such countries feel that the standard limits are adequate.

6. In the Netherlands, nontariff insurers write most long-term policies. Their attitude toward cancellation contrasts with their liberality in other matters.

7. Italian insurers eliminate this restriction for insureds which buy an endorsement costing from 10 to 20 percent of the base premium.

8. While insuring on the basis of replacement cost is the liberal practice, not all corporate property owners which are eligible for the plan choose to use it, for it necessitates maintaining larger amounts of insurance than under actual cash value, thereby entailing higher premiums and increased exposure to coinsurance penalization.

9. In most countries, premium rates applicable to replacement cost policies are no higher than those of actual cash value policies; the larger amounts of insurance purchased under replacement cost provide insurers with the amounts of money they need to pay the larger losses inherent under the plan.

10. Conceivably, through integration of national markets via the European Economic Community and the Andean Common Market, revenue flows might become sufficiently concentrated to permit correction of the deficiencies.

11. Even more annoying are markets in which domestic insurers are free of competition from each other as well as from foreigners. The complacency and laziness afflicting insurers operating without competition preclude the production of improved plans of protection.

12. Despite the implied exclusion of brokerage, the Italian government does not close the market to domestic brokers completely.

13. For ten years, a government-organized cartel operated in Germany. Its membership included all insurers in the market other than a few admitted foreigners, and all members observed tariffs without deviation. Since 1973, however, German tariffs have been advisory only.

14. "Housekeeping" here means orderliness and cleanliness in use and maintenance of property.

15. Consideration here is limited to primary insurers. Had reinsurance specialists been included, companies in several other countries would have been indicated.

16. In some countries, corporate users of insurance are not annoyed by the fact that

their premium rates reflect high costs of reinsurance. They are aware that the reinsurers are providing dependable protection while their primary insurers may pay tardily or not at all.

17. Although greater amounts of liability insurance are sold in the United Kingdom on the nontariff basis than in any of the countries listed above, much is sold also in the tariff market.

18. Danish insurers carry the indexing approach to the ultimate by specifying no limits of protection in their policies. Premiums are based upon the most recent evaluations of the covered property, but recoveries are based upon replacement cost as of the dates of loss.

19. Indicative of the difficulty of providing adequate limits is the contrast between the Japanese government's eagerness for foreigners to provide earthquake insurance and its reluctance to permit them to cover other perils.

9

COPING WITH AGGRESSION AND OTHER CONDITIONS OVERSEAS

Most of the risk control measures employed by foreign affiliates of American owner corporations are much like those used in the United States. There are some, however, which have no counterparts in this country. Described below are the more notable of these practices and the bases for deciding when they should be used.

Meeting the Extortion Risk

Extortion, by kidnapping or threatening bodily harm, has been practiced since men first coveted the clubs, flints, pelts, caves, and wives of other men. Since the late fifties, however, it has become a much more costly crime than ever before for American corporations operating in other countries. On all continents, managers have become aware that they or their associates may be kidnapped and even killed in extortionate moves against their employers.

In some of the cases, the extortionists were common thieves motivated solely by avarice; in others, bands of kidnappers or assassins sought funds for financing revolutionary activity. In all cases, however, the managers of the target companies knew that the criminals were prepared to commit murder. Typically the amount of the ransom or the award for refraining from assassination has been high. In thirty extortionate attacks in twelve countries from midyear 1972 to the end of 1973, the average demand was the equivalent of $1,443,000. Thirteen of the victims were employees of affiliates of American corporations. Because inflation will affect extortion payments at least as much as other casualties, future losses can be expected to rise substantially.

Basic Decisions

The first step in coping with the risk of extortion loss is establishment by the board of directors of the policy the corporation will follow in response to assassination threats or demands for ransom. The board can direct management to refuse to pay under any circumstances, to comply completely with demands, or to exercise its judgment in each situation as to whether or not to pay. Directors face no responsibility with a greater potential for anguish; whatever their decision, murder of employees may follow.

The corporate policy prohibiting payment to extortionists rests on the belief that surrender to demands will lead to additional threats; a corollary belief is that the owner company is so widely exposed to extortion that it must reject all demands flatly. Otherwise, according to this reasoning, the company's reputation of concern for the safety of all of its employees may cause extortionists to assume that they could obtain equally large amounts of money by threatening to kill rank-and-file employees. The conclusion, therefore, is that announcing unequivocally that the company will not comply with extortionate demands is more likely to discourage kidnapping or assassination than the other forms of response.[1]

In its second move, the board of directors decides whether foreign affiliates are to publicize the planned modes of response. If corporate policy requires the affiliates to refuse to pay any amount, logic indicates that local managers should announce the policy and indicate that they will implement the order, however tragic the consequences may be. Possibly, of course, strategy will fail if the extortionists believe that the directors will capitulate under stress.

If policy requires foreign affiliates either to pay as demanded or to respond as they see fit, it also should direct local managers to confine knowledge of the decision to the very few employees who would be involved in dealing with the extortionists. Otherwise, word of the readiness to pay will soon reach those who may take advantage of what they regard as weakness. Secrecy will not necessarily prevent prospective extortionists from attacking, but it is more likely to do so than acknowledgement that management has been authorized to pay if it feels that it must.

Corporate directors also must decide whether use of insurance is an appropriate means of controlling the peril. Ordinarily, board members do not ponder insurance matters, but many of them feel that they must make the decision as to whether their companies should use extortion insurance for it is literally of life or death significance. Specifically, they fear that executives will be murdered because their companies use the insurance or because they do not use it. They ask management for advice but are never certain that they have made the right decision.

Management's responsibilities are to devise methods of frustrating kidnappers and assassins and to fund such efforts. This is not an area of casualty prevention in which experience and conscientious effort automatically bring success; success in shielding employees from kidnappers and assassins may be due mainly to luck. Managers are aware of this but must devote to it the amounts of thought and money they would employ if they were certain that their efforts would be successful.

Kidnapping and Assassination Prevention

Although an executive who is aware that he may be kidnapped and assassinated adopts protective measures of his own devising, much more than his sporadic and intuitive efforts are necessary. Managers of the owner corporation and the affiliate must work with him and with consultants or in-house specialists in extortion prevention. Management of the owner corporation establishes policies such as the following; local managers are to cultivate low profiles in their communities; local managers are to refrain from discussing with employees or outsiders the ties to the owner corporation; the affiliate's name is not to indicate the relationship to the owner corporation; as many nationals as possible are to hold managerial positions; American executives or technicians are to visit the affiliate as infrequently as possible.

The implementation of such policies is a responsibility of the affiliate's management. Thus, local managers rarely offer statements to reporters and make no speeches off company premises. They do not provide newspapers or periodicals with their photos or biographical data. They attempt to induce employees and outsiders to overlook any relationship with any owner corporation.

In the main, local management faces an almost impossible task. Concealment of the prosperity of a city's largest employer, of the foreign influence upon the company, or of the identity of key employees is impossible. If, however, a company has made itself less conspicuous than others in its area, it may win a low position on extortionists' lists of targets.

Preventive facilities

To ward off kidnappers and assassins, management hires bodyguards and installs protective equipment. If a pattern of extortion in the affiliate's country indicates that extortionists move against only top executives, it may be necessary to assign them bodyguards.

Bodyguards cannot provide total protection against political terrorists but, if well trained, they reduce terrorists' probabilities of success and almost eliminate any threat of extortion by the common criminals.

Protective equipment consists of weapons and devices installed in offices, homes, and autos. Used in working places are such protections as alarm systems, plexiglass window panes, dead-bolt locks, and elevators accessible only to executives. A home can be equipped with barred windows, one-way peepholes in doors, a radio transmitter (for calling for help if telephone lines should be cut), heavy window curtains, and fire extinguishers capable of smothering flaming gasoline bombs. Also desirable in many cases are alarm systems. Some systems warn of the presence of fire or intruders; others alert patroling police or private guards to break-ins by lighting windows which otherwise are always dark or by lighting windows in certain patterns. In contrast to installing such equipment is the removal of large trees and dense shrubery which could conceal assassins or kidnappers.

Executives' autos can be armored against pistol and rifle fire. However, their large size and the thickness of their window panes make them easily identifiable even in dense traffic, and, further, the armor does not withstand armor-piercing shells. More useful than bulletproofing, therefore, is equipping vehicles with transmitters for summoning police.

Disciplines

At least as necessary as use of protective equipment by the executive and his family is their observing of certain disciplines. If he drives to work, the executive must use a variety of routes, and in leaving his home or office he must not indicate his planned route to his secretary or other employees. If he uses any of several routes, the law of averages offers some assurance that assassins or kidnappers will not correctly predict his random choice.

Whenever he drives, he must assume that extortionists may attempt to compel him to stop, or to reduce speed by blocking him front and rear, or to force him off the road. Kidnappers need halt him only for seconds in order to seize him, and assassins can shoot or firebomb him while in motion. Therefore, he searches his mirror continually for vehicles trailing at unusually short distances and is ready at any moment to swerve sharply to escape.

Upon arriving at his working place, he parks in a restricted area in view of an attendant he recognizes. If possible, he enters the building in the company of persons with whom he works.

As a self-disciplined executive he foregoes the managerial privilege of working in the office during evenings, Sundays, and holidays. An executive in a nearly deserted street, parking structure, office building, or laboratory can be an easy target.

Fully as necessary as disciplined behavior on the part of executives is the caution on the part of supervisors. Personnel managers, for example, hire applicants only after screening them for evidence of sympathy with terrorist groups. Nevertheless, other supervisors must assume that sympathizers can have slipped through the screening and must recognize the need to withhold from almost all employees any news of coming events which may offer opportunities for kidnappings or murders. They protect key persons by confining knowledge of travel plans, meetings, vacations, and transfers to the very few employees who are necessarily involved in the moves. They routinely conceal memoranda, reports, letters, telegrams, and cablegrams. When possible they refrain from engaging in telephone discussions of impending travel, meetings, or changes in personnel, lest they reveal information to impostors or line tappers.

Security also requires that management enforce rules barring from company premises persons not known to guards; likewise, it forbids the hiring of strangers for temporary assignments and sometimes bars the temporary shifting of employees. Illustrative of the need for prohibiting practices as commonplace as making temporary reassignments is the unintended release of news by a member of a typing pool who substituted for a secretary for two days and thereafter chatted innocently but dangerously about her glimpse of the president's fascinating activities, including the three-country trip which he would soon make.

Extortionists do not attack only executives, nor do they attack only during business hours. Consequently, the executive and the other members of his family must observe discipline in their personal activities. Mainly, they deny themselves simple pleasures. Thus, they do not stroll in their neighborhood or hike in the mountains. Rarely do they make casual evening visits or attend theatrical performances or dine out. The children do not ride bicycles to school with their friends, traveling instead in cars driven by bodyguards or alert servants.

In the home, the family functions much as a group under siege. The children cannot answer telephone questions as to the whereabouts of their father or the probable time of his arrival at any destination even when they are certain that they recognize the caller's voice. The wife must either assign grocery shopping to a servant or make shopping trips under guard. If she shops in person, she must do so at varying times of the day lest a pattern of travel be detected by extortionists.

No member of the family can respond to the ring of a doorbell by simply opening the door. Instead, the caller is viewed through a peephole and the door is kept closed to a stranger—however innocent in appearance. And instead of eagerly tearing the wrappings of incoming packages or hastily slitting bulkly envelopes, family members must regard such items as explosive devices until they know them to be harmless.

The presence of wary servants is a near necessity of life under such conditions. Indeed, in no other household process is greater care needed than in hiring domestics. The backgrounds of applicants must be studied by police or by private investigators. Moreover, even if the family has confidence in the servants' integrity, it must not overlook that the possibility a loyal employee can release, unthinkingly, information which can reach extortionists. Therefore, the family does not discuss, in the presence of servants, matters it does not want known by extortionists.

Effectiveness of efforts to prevent extortion loss

Ideally, extortion prevention programs are so formidable that they deter extortionists. Some programs may have had that effect, but management cannot assume that its preventive measures have negated the risk of extortion. At any time, a group may decide that its advantages as an aggressor are more potent than the defenses of the target company. It is certain that neither the police nor the company has its operatives under surveillance. It builds self-confidence by reminding itself that an offensive force can attack when it pleases, can postpone an attack at the last moment to avoid disaster, and can seize unexpected opportunities to capture or kill. It prides itself that its members are indifferent to the possibility that they will be killed in action. If it already is well financed, it exults in possessing whatever equipment it may need to pierce armor on vehicles or to break into buildings.

The extortionists' confidence is further bolstered by the knowledge that a management caught between regard for human life and responsibility for earning profits and preserving assets may act uncertainly. The leaders guess that management's determination to save employees' lives may end in yielding when firm refusal to pay up might have won the day. They assume also that pressure to maximize profits has forced management to spend so little to protect employees that their attacks cannot fail.

Seemingly, the advantages held by extortionists, when combined with fierce determination, loom above the defensive equipment and protective disciplines of the target corporation and its executives. If this depressing observation is accurate, the corporation must adopt a military approach if it is to prevent kidnappings and assassinations.[2] Confronted by a paramilitary force, it can prevail only by countering with military techniques and attitudes. The techniques would include such measures as employing large numbers of trained guards and undercover agents, infiltration, and close association with local and national police. The most important attitude would be acceptance of whatever costs for whatever number of years might be necessary to outlast tenacious and resourceful enemies.

Insuring against Extortion

A consideration underlying every decision to buy extortion insurance is the amount of the possible loss. Although the underwriters who head the Lloyd's syndicates writing most of the world's extortion insurance have accumulated data regarding payments made to extortionists by the syndicates and by victimized companies directly, they do not publish it in detail. Presumably they refrain lest they contribute to the expansion of extortion by publicizing its profitability. Nevertheless, sketchy indications of amounts paid to extortionists suggest that in several countries the extortion risk produces losses second in average size only to those caused by fire. Aware of their exposure to loss of as much as $10,000,000 in a single incident, numerous owner corporations have chosen to insure.

In the opinion of brokers specializing in securing extortion insurance, the fear board members and members of top management have of kidnapping is another basis for deciding to use such protection.[3] Directors, in particular, view the horrors inherent in kidnapping and assassination with dismay. Consequently many have directed their companies to insure in order to assure availability of adequate cash in the event of kidnapping or threat of assassination.

Probably a majority of directors of risk control disagree with board members and top management as to the desirability of using extortion insurance. They do not argue that extortion is a peril of little significance, but they assign lower priorities to extortion insurance than to other needs for insurance. One, for example, believes that courts in several of the countries in which his company has affiliates soon will be awarding damages more frequently and in much larger amounts than in the past. He feels, therefore, that the affiliates should greatly increase their liability insurance limits. Conversely, while he knows that a kidnapping or a threat of assassination could result in a loss exceeding a million dollars, he knows also that the probability that any of the affiliates ever will incur such a loss is very low. In his opinion, then, if the company is to increase its spending for insurance, it should buy additional liability protection before it secures extortion insurance.

The extortion insurance market

Extortion insurance was first offered by Lloyd's underwriters in 1973. Within two years, two American carriers entered the market. By mid-1975, brokers regarded the compact market as stable and dependable, noting that the insurers had canceled few policies, if any, and were willing to write protection in all countries.[4]

Policy provisions

Provisions of extortion policies are concise, free of ambiguities, and few in number. In outlining the insurer's basic obligations, an insuring agreement provides for indemnification of insureds after they have paid ransom to kidnappers of "insured persons," defining that term as either "all individuals listed . . . in the declarations" or "any member of the insured's organization specified . . . including all members of, or guests (in) his/her household, and relatives."

Originally, the policies applied only to extortion through kidnapping. With assassination threats producing payments fully as large as ransoms, the protection was inadequate, and insurers either broadened their insuring agreements to include also "the receipt of a threat to kill or injure an insured person" or added endorsements to that effect.

The liability of the insurers under all extortion policies is measured in terms of "ultimate net loss," defined as "the sum of monies or the monetary value of any other consideration which the insured shall finally have paid/delivered, after all recoveries made thereafter have been taken into account." Obviously, if insurers defer indemnification until all possibilities of recoupment through apprehension of the extortionists have passed, most insureds will wait for recovery for many months.

The provisions defining conditions precedent to recovery are as clear as the insuring agreements. The number of conditions vary with the insurers, but during the late seventies the policies of the three insurers required that (a) the recipient of a threat of assassination or of harm to a kidnapped person must notify a member of the employer's top management and (b) the employer must promptly notify the police of the threat. Each policy also included one or more of these conditions: (a) a recipient of a threat of assassination or of harm to a kidnapped person must ascertain that the threat was genuine; (b) the insured company must have established a procedure for verification of threats by its senior officers; (c) those who arranged for payment to extortionists must have recorded serial numbers of bills; (d) management must have made every reasonable effort to conceal the existence of the policy from all but a necessary few of its members.

The requirement of concealment sets the extortion policy apart from all others. Based on the assumption that widespread knowledge of a company's insurance protection might lead to an extortion attempt, it seems to meet the approval of American owner corporations. Indeed, some probably are more secretive than their insurers had hoped. For example, in a corporation having affiliates in numerous countries, only the members of the board of directors and the president, the vice president (finance), the vice president (international), and the director of risk control know of the corporation's extortion policy. Unaware of it are the corporation's accountants and the managers of the affiliates who are named in the policy as "insured persons."

In keeping with the simplicity of the insurers' obligations, the policies include few or no specific exclusions. By implication, however, requirements that the insurers be reimbursed for money paid in swindles perpetrated by officers of insured companies in connection with real or spurious kidnappings or assassination threats are exclusions.[5] Otherwise, the only exclusions apply to unusual local situations.

The only provision aimed at protecting the insurer against adverse selection (i.e., the insuring of an abnormally high proportion of substandard risks) is a warranty holding that the corporation has received no threats of kidnapping or assassination during the twelve months preceding the policy's inception date. If the policy did not include the warranty, an extortion insurer would be operating in approximately the manner of a health insurance company which issues hospital-medical policies to persons who apply for the protection en route to the hospitals where they are to undergo surgery. Nevertheless, the American insurers ordinarily do not insist upon inclusion of the warranty. Presumably, they feel that a device for coping with adverse selection would be of little worth in an area of risk in which adverse selection does not occur in the ordinary sense of the term, inasmuch as virtually all the insureds—in certain countries, at least—are exposed to loss.

Decision making by prospective insureds

Ordinarily, the buyer of extortion insurance chooses between per-incident limits of protection of $1,000,000 or $5,000,000 and aggregate limits of $3,000,000 or $10,000,000.[6] Three considerations underlie its choices, the recent history of extortionate acts in the countries of its affiliates having the most weight. If extortionists have forced companies in some of the countries to surrender amounts in excess of $1,000,000 and if demands are rising, limits of $5,000,000 and $10,000,000 clearly are indicated. Also considered are the sizes of the owner corporation and the affiliates. Large affiliates of giant owner corporations are subjected to much higher demands than smaller companies, and they need the highest limits available. The least important of the considerations is the cost of the insurance. Premiums vary, of course, with policyholders' exposure to risk. The range of charges for $5,000,000 and $10,000,000 limits is approximately $50,000 to $120,000 per year. Premiums for $1,000,000 and $3,000,000 limits are only slightly lower than the bottom of that range; while most of the affiliates covered under the lower limits are relatively small, they are located in countries in which attacks can be expected each year. Paying the highest premiums are corporations operating large affiliates in dozens of countries, including the three or four which are notorious for extortionate activity.

Insuring against extortion loss requires decisions as to countries and persons to be covered. Commonly, management wants the protection to apply only to the few countries in which extortion clearly is an active peril. Thus, a corporation having affiliates in 35 countries may wish to insure affiliates in only five of the countries. However, because the insurer does not yet have credible loss data, it may demand that its coverage blanket all the countries in which the owner corporation has affiliates. The premiums applicable to low-hazard countries, it hopes, will compensate for any inadequacies in premiums applicable to high-hazard countries.

Even if the insurer does not demand such breadth of coverage, the owner corporation may request it, knowing that terroristic extortion can occur in any country. In every country are persons equipped with the requisite ruthlessness and contempt for the concept of individuals' rights to live and to own property. Moreover, extortionists are not confined by national borders and at any time can make forays into countries which have been relatively free of their attacks.

The principal question as to employees to be covered is whether protection is to apply to all employees or only to employees listed in a schedule. Both insurers and insureds have mixed feelings on the subject. The former prefer the broad premium base which develops from coverage of all employees but recognize that employers cannot physically protect all their employees. The insureds know that extortionists conceivably will move against any of their employees but fear that insuring against attacks upon low-level managers or rank-and-file employees might increase the frequency of such acts. In fact, however, the employer which has a choice need not spend much time in pondering. To list by guesswork the names of employees who might become victims is an exercise surpassed in futility only by an attempt to predict the employees who might steal from their employers. Any employee can steal from his employer; any employee can be attacked by extortionists. Unless an extortion policy applies to all employees, therefore, it is defective. Moreover, unless a clear trend toward attacking low-level employees develops, the added cost of covering all employees will not be much over 15 percent.

Policyholders' decisions regarding deductibles may have considerably greater effects upon premiums than decisions regarding numbers of employees to be covered. All extortion policies include either fixed-amount deductibles or percentage-participation provisions. Ordinarily, the insured can select the amount of its per-incident, fixed-dollar deductible from a range of $10,000 to $100,000, choosing most commonly $25,000 or $50,000. In some cases, however, insurers permit no such elections, requiring instead that the insureds bear, in each loss, either 5 percent or a fixed amount such as $25,000.

Regardless of which party to the policy decides upon the form and amount of the deductible, the plan is almost certain to be speculative from the insured's standpoint.[7] If, therefore, the owner corporation can choose its deductible amount, its choice should be consistent with its decisions as to use of speculative deductibles elsewhere in its insurance program. If it feels comfortable under large, speculative deductibles in policies resembling extortion contracts in prospective frequencies of loss and in premium rate credits, it should place such a deductible in its extortion policy. Otherwise, given the evolutionary status of this area of risk, it probably should employ the minimum acceptable to the insurer.

Finally, with regard to policy provisions, the insured must decide whether or not to buy protection against secondary perils. Under one supplementary cover, the insurer will reimburse kidnapped or threatened employees for payments by them or members of their families out of personal resources. If this extension were not in the policy, the insurer would not indemnify an executive or members of his family for such payments. Moreover, because the demands were not directed to the employer, it would not compensate the employer for voluntarily reimbursing the employee or his family.

Clearly, the employer which insures against extortion should provide financial protection to the employees. If risk of loss of life is a part of a job, the responsible employer makes every reasonable effort to protect the employee. If by prompt delivery of its own money the terrorized family of a kidnapped executive saves his life, the employer's insurance should cover the ransom as fully as if the employer had delivered the funds. Endorsement of this extension to a policy does not increase the premium inasmuch as it does not add to the policy's limit of liability.[8]

Another extension applies to extortionate threats to damage buildings and the contents thereof. Political terrorists began burning and blasting corportions' property before they added kidnapping and threat of assassination to their repertoire. Until the early seventies, however, they were content to destroy property in order to disrupt production and frighten employees into resigning. With increased need of funds, some changed their tactics, threatening to burn or bomb property unless they received cash.

Under the property damage endorsement, a company which has paid extortionists to refrain from destroying its property is indemnified. This endorsement is not likely to be widely used. Criticism of it is based mainly on the assumption that attempts to buy good behavior would result in ever larger numbers of threats; extortionists who may hesitate to kill or kidnap may not be at all reluctant to destroy property.

Extortion insurance in the future

During the first three years of experimenting with extortion insurance, many of those involved in selling and servicing the protection felt that its period of use would be brief. Aware of management's uncertainty as to its worth and of the insurers' apprehensions, they assumed that demand soon would evaporate or the market would close down. By 1976, however, they had begun to feel that the new plan of insurance would be offered and used indefinitely. They foresaw no end to extortion for either political purposes or personal gain and were becoming confident that insureds' programs for preventing kidnapping and assassination would prevent losses from soaring unpredictably.

However, the directors of risk control who had opposed purchase of the protection tended to believe that top management would decide against paying extortion premiums after five or six loss-free years.

Coping with Expropriation and Other Perils

The belief that national objectives justify whatever means might lead to attainment subjects every American corporation doing business abroad to perils known as "political contingencies."

The most formidable of them is expropriation, i.e., seizure of all the assets of a company. Occurring sometimes as a prelude to expropriation and sometimes as an unrelated violation of property rights is confiscation—seizure of portions of the victim's assets. Unlike expropriation, confiscation does not necessarily force the victim to halt its operations. Another sanction bars remittance of a company's profits to the alien owner corporation. Still another repudiates contracts for supplying goods or services. For example, a government cancels a a contract with a construction firm to design and build a nuclear power plant. Having spent heavily in planning and in acquisition of equipment, the contractor incurs a large loss.

"Creeping nationalism," a term coined by Lloyd's underwriters, refers to aggressive governmental moves against particular companies, such as imposing discriminatory taxes on property, requiring employment of nationals whether or not they are qualified for their jobs, ordering wage increases whether justified by productivity or not, and discriminatorily freezing prices. Eventually, those forms of interference can force foreign owner corporations to sell their affiliates to the domestic government or to corporations owned by nationals.

The war damage peril, too, is included in the list of political contingencies. Civil or international wars are in progress somewhere almost any day. They constitute the ultimate in coercion and qualify, therefore, for inclusion.

Mainly, political contingencies entail governmental acts, but some of those who seize property and otherwise interfere with business operations are revolutionaries and some are privateers licensed explicitly or implicitly by governments. Whether governmental or private, political aggressors can destroy their victims.

Amounts of Loss

Conceivably, expropriation could be financially beneficial to an owner corporation. If its affiliate faced a high probability of large losses indefinitely but the owner nevertheless continued to operate it because of pressure from government or from conscience, the prospective operating loss might exceed the loss through expropriation of assets.

Almost always, however, expropriation results in severe net losses to owner corporations. Because taking property forcibly, with or without compensation, is an almost unbearable affront, top management commonly tries to console itself by observing, in effect, "we retrieved our investment (in the lost company) three times through earnings and should not, therefore, grieve very much." Typically, it bases the retrieval ratio on earnings dollars, which are of much less value, because of inflation, than the dollars invested years earlier, and the ratio does not depict the full amount of the victim's loss. The process, therefore, is one of avoiding the reality of large losses. Such losses are especially large when the expropriators pay only token compensation or none at all. While undervaluing such losses might relieve management's distress, it is at odds with management's responsibility to report accurately to stockholders.

Outlined below is a measurement of the loss inflicted upon the foreign owner of an industrial plant through expropriation by an imaginary government. Magnanimously, the government will pay 80 percent of the plant's book value in six equal annual installments, beginning one month after seizure. The values of the assets are as indicated below.

Book Value	Replacement Cost	Replacement Cost Less Depreciation*
$18,000,000	$32,000,000	$27,546,000

*Depreciation calculated in terms of physical reduction in utility.

Therefore, the government is to pay $14,400,000. The immediate loss to the company, consequently, is the difference between $14,400,000 and the values of the assets in terms of present costs of replacement less depreciation.[9] This loss amounts to $13,146,000. Additional loss, through preclusion of profits, will result from (a) loss of the productivity of assets amounting to $27,546,000 (less the amount to be earned on portions of the $14,400,000 after transfer to other countries), (b) inability to earn elsewhere as much as had been earned in the expropriating country, and (c) the government's decision to pay the $14,400,000 in six annual installments of $2,400,000, with the first payable at once and with no provision for interest on the remaining five. If the affiliate's earnings had amounted to about 10.5 percent of assets (valued at replacement cost less depreciation) and could have been expected to continue at that rate for at least ten more years, assets worth $27,546,000 would have generated profits having a projected value at time of seizure of about $17,397,360. Earnings to be produced by investment in another country of the government's six installment payments at an interest rate of 8.5 percent had a projected value of approximately $6,236,720. Profits precluded, therefore, will equal the difference—$11,160,640.

Not all expropriations, of course, will necessarily be followed by reinvestment of the indemnities at lower rates of return than those earned before the takeovers. Neither, however, will expropriations necessarily be followed by prompt and full payments of the governments' promissory notes. Without question, expropriation must be regarded as a major area of risk for any American corporation maintaining affiliates abroad.

Confiscation and prohibiting remittance of earnings have occurred more frequently than expropriation. Resultant losses of American companies from the first two, however, have not approached the losses from expropriation. Also, most confiscation and inconvertibility losses have occurred as deferrals. After several years of preventing an owner corporation from transporting its affiliate's earnings to the United States, for example, a government permits remittance of some or all of the funds. Similarly, a government which confiscated a shipment of components en route to a company in its country eventually releases it. Under either form of interference, loss can be severe. If the currency of an affiliate's country were to depreciate by 45 percent (in terms of the value of the dollar) during inconvertibility and the government were to permit remittance of only the number of units of currency it had blocked, the erosion of earnings would be substantial. Likewise, if confiscation were to reduce output of an affiliate by 40 percent over a period of 120 days, the loss could be painful.

War, revolution, or insurrection can, of course, result in total loss of industrial or commercial facilities. However, they do not necessarily produce destruction. Revolutionaries who succeed in overthrowing governments prefer expropriation to destruction, and military commanders have ignored looting by their troops while prohibiting the wrecking of factories, refineries, and rolling stock which will be useful to the new governments.

Markets

Governmental and private insurers provide the various forms of political risk insurance. Underwriters at Lloyd's long have written protection against confiscation of and war damage to shipments by sea, but until 1974 they provided expropriation insurance only by reinsuring the Overseas Private Investment Corporation (OPIC), the United States government's agency for providing political contingencies insurance, and similar insurers operated by fifteen other national governments.

OPIC was established in 1969 to take over the insuring function handled for the preceding twenty years by other agencies of the federal government. Congress' main purpose in establishing it was to encourage American companies to make investments in countries in need of capital. A secondary intention was to stimulate companies to increase their volumes of trade with emerging nations and long industrialized countries.

Optimists assumed that OPIC could meet all demands for protection without governmental subsidization. However, by the mid-seventies, its directors and some members of Congress realized that it faced the possibility of large underwriting losses if it were to continue to meet all requests for full coverage of new overseas ventures. Aware that expropriation was regarded by some governments as a more effective means of national development than private saving or taxation, they moved to permit OPIC to set low ceilings of protection in some countries and to include deductibles in its policies.

By 1975, OPIC had evolved into a unique, voluntary combination of governmental and private insurance facilities. Adding to its capacity for providing expropriation, confiscation, and inconvertibility insurance was the Overseas Investment Insurance Group (OIIG), composed of Lloyd's syndicates and twelve American insurers. OIIG writes basic covers in amounts up to $6,500,000 per company and OPIC provides as much as $40,000,000 more on the excess basis.

OPIC insures in the manner of surety bonding companies. As sureties recover whatever they pay in consequence of defaults by their bonded customers (if all goes well), OPIC recovers in full from governments the amounts it has paid policyholders which were barred from remitting earnings or suffered confiscation or expropriation of assets. It has been particularly successful in obtaining reimbursement of amounts it has paid to companies which were unable to remit earnings, recovering 98 percent of such payments during the period 1971–74.

With OPIC barred, prior to 1974, from insuring long established commercial or industrial operations anywhere or new facilities in countries having a per capita gross national product of over $1,000, thousands of American corporations having affiliates abroad had no way of insuring against political contingencies until Lloyd's and American International Group began responding to their needs.[10] Entry into that field reflected much courage, for they had almost no historical data upon which they could base policy clauses and premium rates. OPIC's experience afforded little guidance, inasmuch as it related to political climates in newly emerging countries and to attitudes of governments toward an insurer which was an agency of the government of the United States, not a private company. Nevertheless, by mid-1976 more than 100 Lloyd's syndicates were participating in the new plan, led by two which were writing about 20 percent of each risk. The participating syndicates had long been active mainly in ocean marine insurance, wherein they had written more war damage protection than any other carriers. After two years of experimenting, the underwriters were still far short of their objective of basing their risk taking upon surpluses extracted from profits rather than from the syndicates' members. Nevertheless, they were committing themselves to per-country limits of protection as high as $162,000,000.

The Covers

Ordinarily, the insurers constituting the private market for political risks insurance are not in competition with OPIC and its counterparts in other governments. Corporations do not choose between the two markets on the basis of difference in policy provisions. Therefore, the following comparison of policy provisions offered in the markets is a means of describing the various provisions, not an indicator of choices to be made.

The private carriers insure against loss by expropriation, confiscation, inconvertibility of earnings, and creeping nationalism.[11] Also, they bear losses resulting from the overt forms of aggression, i.e., destructive acts by rioters, other violent persons, and military forces. However, by mid-1978, their war damage insurance applied only to property in transit, such as shipments between owner corporations and affiliates.[12]

The Lloyd's syndicates much prefer protecting against expropriation and confiscation to covering inconvertibility of earnings. Possibly, therefore, a company in need of a high limit of inconvertibility protection will not be able to buy it. Completely unavailable is protection against loss through depreciation of domestic currencies during blockage. Thus, a company recovers from its insurer the amount of money which had been blocked, whatever the depreciation of the currency before receipt of the payment.

Covered by the private insurers on the supplemental basis are creeping nationalism and loss of net profits from confiscation or expropriation. Under creeping nationalism endorsements, insurers indemnify companies which, for example, have been forced to promote unqualified nationals and have incurred losses thereby. Net profits endorsements indemnify insureds for short- or long-term reductions in earnings due to expropriation or confiscation. Recoveries cannot exceed 25 percent of the policies' basic expropriation or confiscation limits. Consequently, long-term profit losses like that of the illustration above are not likely to be covered in full.

OPIC's coverage now is much like that of the private insurers, including confiscation, expropriation, inconvertibility, and damage by war, revolution, and insurrection. It provided protection against the latter three perils before Lloyd's began to do so and, unlike Lloyd's, does not exclude damage in wars in which specified countries are engaged.

In order to develop the premium volume they deem necessary for bearing large political contingencies losses, Lloyd's underwriters press their policyholders to insure their facilities in all the countries in which they conduct operations. (They provide this breadth of protection by listing in the policy each affiliate and the amount of its insurance.) Conversely, inasmuch as OPIC must focus upon property in countries which have urgent need of foreign investment and has few policyholders operating only in such countries, it does not require that each policy blanket all the foreign locations of the insured.

The periods of time covered under Lloyd's and OPIC policies differ greatly. Lloyd's policies usually apply for one year, while OPIC's standard term is twenty years. (Where conditions are especially hazardous, OPIC writes expropriation insurance for periods of only twelve years.) Because of that difference and because neither reserves the right to cancel the policies, Lloyd's is much better positioned to use expirations for raising premium rates or terminating relationships where probabilities of political aggression are high. Ordinarily, however, the underwriters feel that they have moral obligations to renew policies, and few insureds fear that they will be denied renewal on the ground of increased probability of expropriation. The insureds expect, of course, that renewal premium rates under such circumstances will rise. Also reducing the significance of the difference in duration of protection is OPIC's movement toward reserving the right to raise premium rates or reduce amounts of protection after policies have been in effect for five years.

The insurers differ substantially in their attitudes toward deductibles. The private carriers require that policyholders absorb at least 10 percent of each loss. They do so because of uncertainty about the adequacy of premium rates, not to minimize premiums. OPIC is less demanding, requiring deductibles only if it faces high probabilities of expropriation losses, after having paid such losses recently. Thus, it might require a deductible in a policy applicable to a major mining operation obviously coveted by an acquisitive government.

The basis of valuing expropriation loss used by both OPIC and the private carriers indicates that the insurance is designed not to enable the owner corporation to re-establish the seized facilities but to salvage part of its investment. Ordinarily, expropriation insurers pay current market values of land and costs of replacement of buildings, equipment, and inventories, less book values of depreciation. Because depreciation for book purposes almost always exceeds actual reduction in utility, the owners recover considerably less under their policies than they would have recovered had their plants been destroyed by fire.

Premium rates for the combination of expropriation, confiscation, and inconvertibility vary widely in the private markets. The range seems to be from .2 percent to 10 percent of the values of the covered property, and the average—assuming applicability of a policy to operations in about twenty countries—is approximately 6 percent. OPIC originally charged a uniform rate of .6 percent for the standard trio of covers, a practice consistent with its benevolent purpose. However, the distaste prevailing in Congress during 1974 and 1975 for the prospect of having to appropriate funds to cover prospective deficits led to OPIC's raising its rates to levels as high as 5 percent.

Considerations in the Use of Political Risks Insurance

While management cannot make its decision to use or reject extortion insurance without noting the possibility that insuring would increase the probability of murder of employees, it can concentrate on economic considerations in deciding whether to insure against political risks. Nevertheless, the decision may be a difficult one. While use of such protection may be consistent with the corporation's policy of insuring against damage by fire and other physical damage perils, additional factors should be considered. Illustrative are circumstances of the American owner corporation of a company abroad employing assets worth $30,000,000. The premium rate quoted for insuring the affiliate against loss from expropriation is high—6 percent annually. If the owner does not buy the insurance and expropriation occurs during the seven-year period which it regards as critical, the results will be as shown in Table 1.

Table 1
CONSEQUENCE OF DOING WITHOUT EXPROPRIATION
INSURANCE
COSTING 6 PERCENT

If expropri- ation without compensation occurs in:	Gross loss ($)	Cumulative savings through investment at 8 percent of money not spent for insurance (after tax)*($)	Reduction in income tax in consequence of unindemnified casualty ($)	Net Loss ($)
1 year	30,000,000	974,938	14,400,000	14,625,062
2 years	30,000,000	1,990,433	14,400,000	13,609,567
3 years	30,000,000	3,048,173	14,400,000	12,551,827
4 years	30,000,000	5,191,515	14,400,000	10,408,485
5 years	30,000,000	6,382,420	14,400,000	9,217,580
6 years	30,000,000	7,622,866	14,400,000	7,977,134
7 years	30,000,000	8,914,915	14,400,000	6,685,085

*The annual premium is the net cost which would have been incurred under federal income taxation.

Thus, in this situation of doing without high-cost insurance, the corporation faces a possible maximum net loss of $14,625,062, and, if expropriation were to occur at the close of the seventh year, a net loss of $6,685,085. If the period were to elapse without expropriation, cumulative savings would be $8,914,915.

In the situation of another American owner corporation which likewise is trying to decide whether to insure against expropriation of its $30,000,000 foreign affiliate during the next seven years, the would-be insurer has proposed a premium rate of only .6 percent. If this corporation decides against insuring, its prospects are as indicated in Table 2.

In this situation of doing without low-cost insurance, expropriation in any of the seven years would result in a very large loss. If expropriation did not occur during the period, the gain through avoidance of insurance costs would be only $901,988, the cumulative savings less income tax thereon.

In summary, the maximum possible gain in the high-cost insurance situation amounts to 61 percent of the maximum possible loss. If management believes that the probability of expropriation during the next seven years is very low, it might approve of the speculation which would be involved in doing without insurance.

The prospects in the second situation clearly raise the warning that no company should establish a plan of casualty loss absorption under which it could save little and might lose much. If the company were

Table 2
CONSEQUENCE OF DOING WITHOUT EXPROPRIATION
INSURANCE COSTING .6 PERCENT

If expropri-ation without compensation occurs in:	Gross loss ($)	Cumulative savings through investment at 8 percent of money not spent for insurance (after tax)* ($)	Reduction in income tax in consequence of unindemnified casualty ($)	Net Loss ($)
1 year	30,000,000	97,494	14,400,000	15,502,506
2 years	30,000,000	199,043	14,400,000	15,400,957
3 years	30,000,000	304,817	14,400,000	15,295,183
4 years	30,000,000	519,152	14,400,000	15,080,848
5 years	30,000,000	638,242	14,400,000	14,961,758
6 years	30,000,000	762,287	14,400,000	14,837,713
7 years	30,000,000	891,492	14,400,000	14,708,508

*The annual premium is the net cost which would have been incurred under federal income taxation.

to do without expropriation insurance, its maximum possible gain would be $891,492 and its maximum loss, $15,502,506. If expropriation conceivably could occur in the affiliate's country, management could be charged—justifiably—with failure to protect the interests of the shareholders in doing without insurance.

Two other conditions commonly bear upon decisions as to whether to use political risks insurance. One is the insistence of some members of top management, vice presidents in charge of foreign operations particularly, that the company buy it. In most cases, probably, they are motivated less by economic considerations than by emotional reaction to the aggression inherent in expropriation and the other political contingencies. Whereas corporate directors of risk control may favor absorbing the loss if aggression occurs, top managers may feel that they must take positive action against the perils and therefore order the risk controllers to secure insurance.

The other pertinent condition is the possibility of long delays and costly argument before recovering under the policies. Disagreements between insureds and insurers as to values of expropriated, damaged, or confiscated property are probable; even if major disagreements do not occur, neither the private insurers nor OPIC is likely to pay a large claim in less than a year. While such delays sometimes occur under other kinds of insurance, some in management overlook this and regard the prolonged irritation in effecting recoveries as a cost peculiar to political contingencies insurance.

Coping with Deficiencies of Overseas Insurance Markets

In the opinion of American directors of risk control, many foreign insurance markets offer neither adequate breadth of property damage insurance nor adequate limits of protection against other perils. Outlined below are the prospects of compensating for those deficiencies through use of two forms of insurance designed for that purpose.

"World-wide" Difference in Conditions Policies

Managers of some United States-based corporations accept the opinion of insurers in many other countries that protection against physical damage perils other than fire, explosion, windstorm, and perhaps a few others is unnecessary. Thus, they rely upon the standard property damage policies issued in affiliates' countries and worry only in the still, small hours of the night about the possibilities of damage from perils not covered.

Management in other corporations reasons that unusual perils are no less threatening in other countries than in the United States and directs affiliates to insure with admitted American insurers in their countries which offer broad covers. In still other companies, management insures under the limited covers available in the affiliates' domestic markets and maintains "world-wide" Difference in Conditions insurance to broaden property damage protection.

Brokers and insurers in the international markets disagree as to which of the latter approaches will be the most used. Through future decades, American insurers may be doing business in the markets of almost all countries in which American industrial, commercial, and banking companies operate affiliates and may be free to write whatever breadth of protection they wish. Possibly, too, domestic insurers will be able and willing to write broad coverage. In either case, "world-wide" Diference in Conditions policies would apply only to affiliates in the few countries which had banished American insurers or had forbidden foreign and domestic insurers to write broad coverage. Conceivably, however, by the mid-eighties nationalism may have driven branches, subsidiaries, and fronting associates of American insurance companies from most of the markets of the world.[13] If so, use of "world-wide" Difference in Conditions insurance would be the predominant means of broadening the coverage of foreign affiliates against physical damage perils.

Useful features

As written by insurers in the United States and elsewhere, DIC policies differ considerably in their breadth of protection. Their chief feature in common is their conversion of restrictive, named-perils protection into "all risks" coverage. They cover, that is, all perils which they do not exclude specifically. However, the meaning of "all risks" varies somewhat from one insurer to another. No DIC policy covers every physical damage peril; all name exclusions. The lists begin with the perils covered under whatever standard property damage policies are applicable, continue with perils generally regarded as uninsurable (such as spoilage, wear and tear, electrical surge, and domestic disorders involving military or para-military forces), and conclude with others representative of the individual insurers' special fears. Examples of the third category are water damage from bursting of pipes and collapse of building foundations following erosion caused by the action of waves. Although some DIC policies include numerous exclusions, all apply to many more perils than any policy covering only those designated.

As indicated above, use of DIC policies precludes wastage of premium on overlapping insurance. A company protected under a standard policy against such perils as fire, lightning, windstorm, and vandalism does not buy coverage of those perils in securing DIC. Instead, it buys protection against a limitless number of additional perils.

Another desirable aspect of DIC is the absence of coinsurance requirements. However praiseworthy the coinsurance device is in theory, it is not appreciated by insureds facing large penalties at times of loss. Many American corporations which operate affiliates in other countries are able to defuse coinsurance clauses in policies applicable to their domestic units by cajoling their insurers into including "agreed amount" endorsements or other negating clauses. Insurers in some countries, however, do not, or cannot by law, use such clauses. Consequently, managers of corporations having affiliates in those countries welcome escape from coinsurance complications under the overriding DIC covers.

Variations

As indicated above, a standard "world-wide" DIC policy does not exist. Under the pressures generated by competition and by fear of disastrous losses, the insurers offer enough variety to make comparison shopping worthwhile. To broaden protection, they delete exclusions and add services. Illustrative of the latter is the addition of protection against loss through coinsurance deficiencies under standard policies. If a company covered by this provision were to incur fire loss at a time when the amount of insurance under its standard policy equaled a lower percentage of the value of its property than the required 100 percent, the fire insurer would pay less than the amount of the loss. The DIC insurer thereupon would pay the difference between the value of the damage and the amount of the recovery under the fire policy.[14]

Another example of unusual provisions is coverage of loss from prolonged decline in value of the currency of an affiliate's country (in terms of the United States dollar) during the settling of a claim for fire damage. With the affiliate's fire insurer obliged to pay only the number of units of the domestic currency representing the value of the loss on the day thereof, the recovery in dollars decreases as the settlement process lengthens. Under a DIC policy promising indemnification in such devaluation, the insured avoids this form of loss.

Maximizing benefits

In order that the insured avoid the waste of overinsuring and the penalties for underinsuring, the DIC policy should include a schedule of limits of protection applicable to the affiliates. The limit for a particular affiliate should equal the amount of its fire insurance only if it is exposed to earthquake or flood; those perils, like fire, can cause damage equal to 90 percent or more of the value of its property. Otherwise, DIC limits should be considerably lower than the fire limits. With DIC limits at realistic levels, the owner corporation will pay premiums commensurate with its needs.

In addition to scheduling limits of protection in its policy, the owner corporation must raise the limits as the values of its property increases. While it is not exposed to coinsurance penalization under DIC, it must systematically increase the limits in order to be fully indemnified for large losses. Raising the limits in accordance with indices representing increases in costs of construction and re-equipping might enable the corporation to maintain adequate amounts of insurance. A better approach entails assigning responsibility to the director of risk control for assembling data each month or two on values of the property of each affiliate and raising DIC limits accordingly. In this way the corporation avoids the possibility inherent in use of index numbers that the indices might not closely reflect special features of design and construction in the affiliates' buildings or equipment.

Because DIC policies apply to all physical damage perils not specifically excluded, items in the lists of excluded perils are all important. Obviously, when perils which might produce large losses are excluded, the term "all risks" is less than descriptive. Ordinarily, the shorter the list of exclusions, the more valuable the policy is. Corporations use DIC as protection against costly surprises, and a policy listing only the perils excluded under all DIC policies serves that purpose.

In one kind of situation, however, a director of risk control is justified in insuring with a company which specifies more exclusions than its competitors. If his employer is prepared to absorb losses up to an amount such as $10,000 caused by commonplace perils such as fire, windstorm, or vandalism, it should absorb also losses up to that amount caused by sonic boom, fluids freezing in pipes, rain leaking through skylights, and many other perils. To maximize savings thereby, it should approve of an insurer's excluding perils which cannot produce losses much in excess of $10,000, if the insurer reduces the premium rate adequately.

Usually, the principal contribution of the corporate director of risk control to maximization of the usefulness of DIC is educating managers of foreign affiliates in the worth of such protection. Except for those who have been thus enlightened, chief executives in countries other than the United States and Canada regard DIC as useless and resent their companies' having to pay portions of the premiums. American directors of risk control are not always successful in dispelling the resentment. When local management is especially bitter, the antidote may be to exempt the affiliate from bearing part of the cost of the insurance. If the owner extracts most of the affiliate's earnings, it will recover most of the insurance cost it absorbed by drawing upon earnings reflective of the affiliate's having avoided paying its share.

Finally, among means of drawing maximum benefits from "worldwide" DIC is making certain that the insurer knows of the perils covered by each of the standard policies of the affiliates. Instead of assuming that the insurer has that information, the corporate director of risk control should provide the data and obtain assurance that the DIC premium recognizes the exclusion of perils covered under the other policies. Obviously, if an affiliate in an earthquake zone holds a policy applying specifically to earthquake, a DIC insurer would charge appreciably less than if it alone were to provide the protection.

"World-wide" Excess Policies

The probability that an American corporation's foreign affiliate will incur a loss much larger than the maximum amount of insurance available in its domestic market has not been high. However, in many countries losses exceeding domestic insurance limits are becoming possible. Particularly low are embezzlement and legal liability limits. Inadequate in some countries are the ceilings on business interruption insurance and on life insurance (for protecting employers against loss through deaths of valuable employees). Necessary for the peace of mind of those in the owner corporation's management who know of such inadequacies is use of "world-wide" excess policies to augment standard protection provided by domestic insurers.

Ideally, such policies would span whatever gaps might occur between amounts of loss and limits of basic policies. During the mid-seventies, insurers offered "world-wide" excess insurance but restricted it, ordinarily, to treating legal liability. However, international insurers are resourceful and responsive to needs and will make "world-wide" multi-perils excess insurance available if they foresee expansion in demand.

Presumably, the policies would indicate the perils covered for each affiliate, the limits of protection, and the limits of the underlying policies. An affiliate might thereby have supplemental protection against legal liability, embezzlement, and robbery in the equivalents of $20,000,000, $9,000,000, and $1,000,000, respectively. Another might have supplementary limits against business interruption and deaths of key employees.

Pricing a policy applicable to affiliates in numerous countries is complicated. In addition to considering the differences in hazards in the countries involved and the limits of protection under both the underlying and the excess policies, the insurer might have to make midterm changes in premiums as limits of underlying covers change. In the age of the computer, however, pricing under such circumstances is mainly a matter of arranging for systematic submission of data.

Unfortunately, computers may never be much value to prospective users of "world-wide," multi-perils excess policies in their efforts to compare prospective benefits with costs, for close measurement—through statistical analysis—of probabilities of occurrence of events which might render underlying policies inadequate may remain beyond computer capability. Occurrences such as landmark awards of damages by courts, statutory changes in damages to be paid under codified limits of liability, increases in wage rates, changing of attitudes of judges toward thieves, inflationary increases in values of property and services, and cataclysmic acts of nature occur erratically.

Probably, therefore, managers of owner corporations will decide whether or not to buy "world-wide," multi-perils excess insurance by comparing their intuitive estimates of the probabilities of such occurrences with the probabilities calculated by the insurers—as indicated by premium quotations. If premium rates seem low in terms of their estimates, the managers will buy the covers.

NOTES

1. In fact, a rigid policy of refusal to reward extortionists cannot guarantee immunity against attacks. Revolutionaries determined to damage a company may mount assaults in order to deprive it of particularly valuable employees by murdering some and intimidating others into quitting.
2. Eventually, perhaps, governments will eliminate the extortion peril. Optimists who expect such reform in the near future, however, are rare.
3. The only other risk which frightens board members into ordering purchase of insurance is that of exposure of corporate officers and directors to legal liability for alleged errors which have brought financial losses to shareholders.
4. Ordinarily, however, the insurers protected operations in Italy and Argentina only if they also were covering the owner corporations in all the other countries in which they operated affiliates.
5. The clauses also require the insured companies to prosecute employees who allegedly have been involved in such fraudulent efforts.
6. The aggregate limit is the cumulative total the insurer would pay toward losses resulting from two or more incidents in a policy year.
7. Indicated in Chapter 2 are the rare circumstances which enable companies to employ deductibles in the certainty that they will save money.
8. Available to individuals who wish to have personal protection against loss to extortionists are policies written independently of the employers' policies, if any. Protection in the amount of $500,000 per incident applicable to individuals domiciled in the United States or abroad costs $300 to $400 per year. Ordinarily, it is used by executives who assume that their employers do not employ extortion insurance and may delay fatally in deciding whether or not to pay ransom.
9. Replacement costs reflect the impacts of inflation, and this concept of depreciation recognizes the realities of shrinking values.
10. Indicative of the shallowness of the market was the fact that a single Lloyd's broker was presenting all the requests for political risks insurance to the Lloyd's underwriters and was therefore the intermediary in the writing of virtually all the political risks insurance being afforded by private insurers.
11. In the words of the Lloyd's confiscation form, the underwriters protect against loss from "confiscation, seizure, appropriation, expropriation, request for title or use or willful destruction, by/under the order of the government (whether civil, military or de-facto) and/or public or local authority of the country in which the property hereby insured is covered by the terms of this wording."
12. Their protection does not apply to wars involving France, Germany, Great Britain, the Soviet Union, the United States, or the affiliate's country.

13. Under a fronting arrangement, the insurer which writes the policy cedes the full amount of the risk to another insurer.

14. The portion of the DIC premium applicable to this benefit should be negligible, for the DIC insurer should anticipate paying no losses. By prodding the insureds to increase the amounts of their fire insurance as the values of their property rise, it would prevent coinsurance deficiencies, for most of the insureds would respond positively. (Most of the property owners which are underinsured in terms of their coinsurance requirements have not deliberately underinsured but have drifted into noncompliance through inattentiveness to increases in the values of their property.)

INDEX

187